HEAVEN'S GOT A PLAN FOR YOU

AN AUTOBIOGRAPHY TO INSPIRE—
GIVING HOPE TO THE BROKEN HEARTED.

TRACEY BROUGH

Printed in China through Red Planet Print Management, Sydney Australia

Published by Author Academy Elite PO Box 43, Powell, OH 43035
www.AuthorAcademyElite.com

Identifiers: LCCN: 2020911884
ISBN: 978-1-64746-343-4 (paperback)
ISBN: 978-1-64746-344-1 (hardback)
ISBN: 978-1-64746-345-8 (e-book)

Available in paperback, hardback, e-book, and audiobook

Photography by Tracey Brough. Cover design by Debbie O'Byrne

Dedication

I sit here and take the deepest breath, knowing it is only by God's grace that I have been able to write this book. With all my heart, I dedicate this book to the lover of my soul, my Jesus, my all. It's been His pursuing love that has carried me through every word of this book and moment of my life. May you be glorified, my Lord.

To my husband, for whom I know it hasn't been easy to walk back through this journey to write my book. I thank you for all your love and support through our thirty years of marriage and walking with me through it. I love you.

My beloved spoke
and said to me, 'Arise, my
darling, my beautiful one,
come with me...'. - Song of Solomon 2:10

My Happily Ever After

Nobody knows how invisible I feel
I longed for a love that made me real
I put on a pretty dress hoping to be seen
But reality speaks that won't be deemed
My heart hides away and believes in the lies
I just want a prince that notices all my cries
My heart sings songs wanting to be loved
But nothing happens and I feel so misjudged
I long to be rescued and whisked up in arms held tight
I don't want to be abandoned and held hostage from the
darkness of the night
This longing it screams, and it won't go away
I don't know where to turn as my heart is in dismay
I hear a voice whisper in the stillness of the night
I have come to rescue you; I am your valiant knight
My heart starts to flutter with love never felt
I cry out to Jesus and I am about to melt
I've longed for this love that never seemed to be filled
I now know why because my heart was not tilled
I now have Jesus and my heart is quite content
Because I will be with Him in eternity where I will be com-
plete and not spent
My happily ever after came and rescued me

Table of Contents

Foreword

This book is written with the highest level of honesty and vulnerability. It is a redemptive story of a life taken from ashes to beauty through a series of dramatic, gut-wrenching, and heart-clenching seasons. It's a story of the compelling love of God and the transforming power of a God who can take brokenness and insecurity and turn them into supernatural boldness and tenacity. Tracey is a living miracle, and this book will shock you, inspire you, warm you, stretch you, and change you from the inside out.

~ Suzie Botross, Discipleship Consultant, Speaker, and Author

Preface

I would like to share the story behind the front cover of my book. My eldest son gave me a lensball on my birthday. I was so keen to experiment with using it, but the day of my birthday was quite grey and overcast. Nevertheless, I prayed and asked God for a beautiful sunset, so I could take some photos. I told God it would be such a special present from Him to have a spectacular sunset. It reached five o`clock in the evening, and it was looking like there was not going to be any picturesque sunset at all. My husband wanted to take me out to dinner at a restaurant near the beach. As we drove to the top of the hill near the restaurant, my jaw nearly dropped to the ground. The sky literally went from grey to a fiery bright orange. Tears fell, and I thanked my Heavenly Father for such a flamboyant gift. On my first trip to the United States of America, I sat beside a lady who I showed the picture of the beautiful sunset taken through the lensball. She asked why I didn't use that photo for the book cover, and that is how the picture became the front cover for my book.

God led me to write this book. I knew it only would be done by his grace because He chose a person who had barely any knowledge with computers to write it. God gave me a dream to write this book against all the odds because I only did through year ten in school. The dream involved me going around the world, sharing my testimony of God's amazing grace and mercy. I want my book to touch hearts in the most broken parts of people's lives. I want to show others that the most broken of souls can be healed and made whole.

I would like to acknowledge my publisher, Author Academy Elite for all the help I needed in publishing my book. I would like to thank my editor, Gailyc Sonia, who would have to be one very patient lady, God bless her soul for the incredible amount of work put into editing my book.

I would like to thank my husband, Wesley, for persevering and picking up many other responsibilities while I have been writing my book. This year has been incredibly hard in many ways, but my husband has walked with me through this journey all the way.

To my precious daughter, Annaleise, without whom this book would not have happened. She has persevered and been by far the most patient person I know. Through all my tears and my one million questions of 'How do I do this?' or 'Can you just do this for me?' she stuck by me all the way. I know there were days you wanted to pull your hair out, but I thank you with all my heart for not giving up on helping me.

To my sons, Benjamin and Joel, thank you for just letting me write this year when I know I had to let things go at home so it could be done. To my youngest daughter Alicia, thank you for the times you spent helping me, as I know this has been an extremely hard year for you.

To my parents, for whom I know this has not been easy either, I thank you both with all my heart. I love you both very much.

To Glenda, my Bible study leader, thank you for your encouragement. You helped me not to give up and always were there for me in my tears and pushed me constantly to get back on my feet. Since I have known you, the love you have shown me has been such a blessing in my life. To the other ladies in my Bible study who have held me in prayer all this year, thank you.

To Ken, pastor at Berwick Church of Christ, thank you for showing me an example of God's true love by shepherding my heart since I came back to Jesus over five years ago now.

To Suzie, who was there with all my questions about publishing a book and giving me advice where needed through this journey, and for writing my forward—thank you.

To Karis, my adopted son in Pakistan, and all my beautiful adopted orphan children in Pakistan, I love you all so much, and I have appreciated all your prayers. Thank you, Karis, for not giving up on me and believing in me against all the odds. I thank your dad and all the people there in the churches who have been praying for me. My prayer is that this book will be translated into Urdu one day and that God will use it to touch many souls there.

To my girlfriend Kay, whom I love dearly, I thank you for not giving up on me and believing in God's grace for this book to be written and the constant encouragement you have given me.

To my Instagram friends who have also kept me in prayers and journeyed with me and to the person who sent the poetry that changed my life, I thank God He used it to bring me closer to Him.

Finally, to Mr. Jack, who is home now in the arms of Jesus, I thank you for telling me I should write a book in the first place. I am sad you are not here to see it, but I know Mrs. Jack is, and you have both been such an encouragement to me most of my life. To another sweet friend Katherine who is also in the arms of Jesus, I thank you for loving me and showing unconditional love since I came back to Jesus. I will never forget you.

••• 1 •••

I Found Jesus—No, I Really Found Jesus

I walked into the church, and I heard the words in my mind, shouting, *I found Jesus!* I thought I imagined it. No, it was getting louder, and my heart was pounding with excitement, illuminated by a bright shining light. I had truly found Jesus—not just asked Him into my heart, but I had discovered who the lover of my soul was, my daddy, my Heavenly Father. I felt like I was walking on a cloud. My walk had a skip in it, and my smile lit up a room. A light had turned on, and Jesus wanted me to know this by those three words. I found Jesus!

I wondered for a minute why I had heard these words so loudly. It felt like all of Heaven was applauding the revelation I had just experienced. Jesus was obviously excited, too, as I could feel His love explode inside me. If I was Jesus, and I had been waiting forty-eight years for me to find myself, I think I would be a tad excited as well. This revelation was so different from when I had first asked Jesus into my heart. There was something so much deeper on all levels. I was experiencing what God had been waiting for in me for many years. He is so patient, so loving, so kind. I know that as a mother, I am not so patient.

After I received the revelation about finding Jesus, I prayed as to why God showed it to me. During the night, I read from the Book of Ezra from the Bible in chapter 6, where it talks about the Jews rebuilding the temple and how they celebrated when it was finished. Straight away, God showed me that is what He was doing the day He divulged that revelation to me. I had a God who delighted in what He saw in me and celebrated the restoration of a once very broken and lost soul. His temple was being rebuilt, Tracey had been restored, and He wanted me to know that.

It had taken me forty-eight years to get to this place of realising I was truly loved finally by someone who would never let me down, never let me go, and love me for who I am—a princess of the one true King, a child of God. My life had changed, with new freedom found in Jesus. Not in my wildest dreams would I have imagined this sort of life even existed. I had not experienced living with such freedom until the last few months of my life.

I walked around like a lovesick child. At first, I thought it was a passing feeling of emotions. I thought I would wake up the next day, and those feelings or experiences would simply disappear, but no. Day after day, things did not change. God was not leaving me, and the change in me was real. I was still getting my mind around what was happening. The love from Jesus I am experiencing was—and still is—overwhelming. It explodes to the point that I beg Jesus to let his love pour out of me into others. I still ask for direction with this newfound love I have. Part of why I am sharing my story in this book is because, with all my heart, I desire for everyone to experience the great love I have found.

I prayed a very bold prayer in January 2019 because I felt so compelled. I asked Jesus to use me all over the world. Crazy, right? Then not long afterward, I was led to write this book. If you only knew the depth of what has brought me to this place. I was a child who thought she was never going to be any good for anyone, a child who felt there was no hope, a child who never dared to dream, and a child who surrounded herself with iron-clad walls so not a soul could get close. That child wanted to experience love, but she could not find it.

Where was God? Did He see her in her childhood when she was sobbing her heart to sleep at night, her pillow soaked with tears? Did He see her aching heart when her parents were continually arguing and fighting? Did He notice her parents were not there for her because of their own painful issues? Where was love? Where was God when she was expected to grow up quickly and take on adult responsibilities? Where was He when she began high school, and she was being teased, left out and bullied, and where she did not fit in. Where was love?

One of my many reasons for writing this book is to get people to see that when we feel totally lost and broken in this world, there is still hope. I noticed something in my life when Jesus was not in it—there was a hole that never seemed to be filled. I thought I could find love in the world by trying to fill the hole with different things. I thought surely there was something that could ease all the years of rejection I had experienced. I mean, I wanted the pain gone. I wanted to be noticed, I wanted to feel loved, so I told myself I was going out into the big world to find it.

Another reason I am sharing my story is that if there is one chance my book stops anyone going through all of what I did, then it has served its purpose. This story is about hope for all who feel it's gone. I walked down some very dark roads in different parts of my life. I speak with confidence, already knowing that when I share my story talking to people on the streets, Jesus uses it to bring down walls. I talk about rejection by my parents as I was growing up and having to grow up at a very young age and be an 'adult'. I recount going through high school, not knowing who I was, being bullied and feeling ugly and never good enough. I did things like cutting myself as a cry for help. My cry to find my identity took me on a forty-eight-year journey. If reading my story trims any time out in someone else's life, then my story serves a purpose. For anyone who has had to walk the road of their parents breaking up, you will find hope in my story. If you are in a struggling marriage, you will learn I relate to your suffering. For anyone who has journeyed through difficult health issues or diseases, you will be encouraged. To those who have lost a child, you will see hope through my story. All the answers to your questions about why such things happen are here for you to read. The many issues I went through will inform and bless you as you read.

Was I scared of writing this book? Yes. Each word written was part of learning to rely on Jesus. I sit and wait. Many times, fear would come, and it stopped me. Sometimes I don't write for weeks. I think there is something to say about putting your heart and your story in a book. You are forced to revisit your past, which brings you to places of healing. When we realise the depth of love Jesus has for us, things start changing, and walls come down. I have never experienced a love so deep. He pursues us, but even when we accept him, He does not stop. I never realised his love does not stop pursuing us while we are here on earth. I recently read the story of Jesus when He crossed the Sea of Galilee. He was exhausted from preaching and doing miracles all day, but He was driven into a boat to pursue a soul possessed by a legion of demons. Who does that? I know after any big event I have finished I'm exhausted, and I want to turn off from the world, never mind travel on a boat to an island to rescue a demon-possessed man! Here is the God who created the world. This is the God who sees our deepest pain and wants to pursue us with all His might to bring us to a place of knowing Him. We will never know or experience the deep love he has for us unless we let Him in.

If we form our opinions based on human love, we will never comprehend His love. As I write now with tears in my eyes, my desire is that through my story, with Holy Spirit-breathed words He has inspired in me, you may discover His love through my journey. To comprehend the love He has had for me is really beyond words, but I'll do my best to relay it. Each day, I discover more and more of who I am in Him. Each day, walls come down, destroying many misconceptions I have of him. Some of this journey is quite painful, but I am after His heart no matter the cost. He gave His all to find me, and He picked me up totally broken. Piece by piece He's making something new; He's making my heart new. To paraphrase the song, 'One Thing Remains' by Jesus Culture, God's love never fails, it never gives up, it never runs out on me. It never stops pursuing us. The comprehension of it is unfathomable. Thank you, Jesus, for not giving up on me.

••• 2 •••

Little Girl's Heart Feeling Lost

One of my earliest memories is of a green tent on a sandy beach, Christie's Beach in Adelaide, South Australia. It turned out it was our home for a few weeks. My dad had no work, and it was the only place we were able to live. There was barely any food to eat, and times were really tough. I imagine this time was very trying mentally and physically on both of my parents. Men in this time of life want to be able to provide, and women like knowing they will be provided for.

As a young child, I had an amazing Nanna. She came to our rescue more times than I could count. This part of my story is hard to talk about but is some of why I am writing my book. My dad was an alcoholic and took drugs. My Dad wasn't at my birth, and I'm told he didn't want me when I was conceived. I believe the alcohol and drugs would have played a part in him not being present at my birth. My mum also didn't want me, as she already had a two-year-old and had recently had a miscarriage before getting pregnant with me. I by no means want to put my parents down; I'm just stating my story through my eyes. Writing about it is not easy. I am revisiting old memories. It's like peeling a Band-Aid off an old wound, but it's one hundred wounds all at once.

When he wasn't drinking, my dad was a really nice man, but when he picked up alcohol, he became an angry, violent drunk. My mum was the one who bore the brunt of this. Many times, her body would be covered in bruises. I knew what had been happening when I saw that. A lot of the bad beatings my mum received were not done in front of us (me or my siblings). They were done behind closed doors. My dad never hit me in his rages of drunkenness. He only hit my mum. One time, my mum nearly lost her life because the beating was so bad. She was in the hospital for days, and her body was black and blue. Despite their problems, I loved both my parents very much.

We used to move from place to place as I was growing up. I found this hard as we never knew where or what we would be living in from one day to the next. I remember living in an upstairs flat in Moorabbin. For some reason, I left the bath running. We were evicted because of that. I can laugh now, but I don't think my parents were laughing back then. We ended up moving around twenty times by the time I had left home. Some of the places we lived weren't exactly homes but literally only a roof over our heads. We lived in tents, caravans, units, flats, houses, bungalows, and even a wardrobe, you name it, we lived in it. We were homeless at times, we barely had money for food a lot of the time, and I do remember those hunger pains.

One of the times my mum had been bashed up, my dad told us to hop into bed and stay quiet. My dad and my brother and sister were also lying on the bed. My dad grabbed my mum's purse and took her last eighty cents. I remember grabbing a necklace she had hidden in there so my dad wouldn't take it, and I hid it in my hand. My dad was insisting we stay silent. I didn't know why until the next minute when there was a tap on the window above our heads. Then suddenly, the window was smashed. It was the police. They had a gun pointed at my dad's head.

This scene was one of those memories I wish could have been erased. It was probably one of the scariest events I recall. My dad had beat up my mum severely, and I remember the police handcuffing him and taking him into a police van—the feeling of standing and watching that left me feeling cold and alone. My mum was gone too, as she had been taken to the hospital. I felt abandoned.

With everything that had happened, my parents ended up getting a divorce, I think I was around five years of age. There is something about wanting my parents to stay together that I longed for. I remember the pain even today. I remember crying myself to sleep many nights and silently praying to God for my parents to get back together. I know many people would have thought it in my parents' best interest for them to get a divorce, but something deeply broke my heart. It hurt deeply, but them being apart broke my heart. It hurt deeply, knowing the love they once had was no more. I never gave up praying. God saw my tears. Nobody else saw how much I wanted my parents back together except Him. I don't remember any other prayers as a little girl, but I do remember that one.

A long journey of being torn between parents started. We would visit my dad on weekends, which ripped my heart apart. I loved my dad. No matter what he had done, I still loved him. There was a deep ache in my heart. I hated the fact that only two out of us three children were allowed to visit at one time on the weekends. I used to try to bribe and beg my mum to let me go with my dad. Many times, my mum would give in and let me go with him. During one of the visits to my dad, on our train ride back home, my heart was sobbing internally. The pain was deep, and I remember my dad's hand around me, holding me close. I loved him, and my heart was breaking to go home without him.

During this time my mum met someone else. As much as I loved my dad, this man brought amazing stability to our lives. We lived in a beautiful house. We had food, and we had a routine. I grew to love this man like a dad. We attended a church Sunday school in Springvale. I attend a primary school in Springvale up until grade three. I remember struggling to fit in with other girls at a young age. I used to hang out with the boys a lot more. There didn't seem to be as much tension playing with boys as with girls. This time in my life seemed stable.

One day something happened. My dad had turned up in a taxi to pick me up, but my mum wasn't home, and I had to make the decision to choose who I would stay with. That may not be significant to anyone else except me, but my heart was being torn. I had to decide—as a five-year-old girl—who I wanted to be with. I remember thinking *Whomever I don't choose will be devastated.* I did end up choosing my dad, but I wouldn't forget having to choose sides. I loved my dad *and* the man my mum was with.

When my dad used to take us for weekends, we would quite often stay in the most random places. Some were really nice, and others you could barely call accommodation. One of the nights I had been with my dad, he had been out drinking, and we had to get a taxi home. I was about five years old, and I had to walk my dad into what felt like a shed. It had a concrete floor with no carpet. There was a wooden door that didn't touch the floor. I remember walking my dad to what looked like a stretcher bed and helped him lay down. I went back to the taxi guy to pay him for the trip. Another time we were getting the train home, and I didn't want to leave my dad. I was sobbing deeply inside my heart but not outwardly showing it. (This memory was one God brought me back to for healing many years later.)

About three years later, my prayers were answered. My parents had started attending a church called the Christian Missionary Alliance in Highett. Then we attended a church called Christian Missionary Alliance Church in Keysborough. My parents ended up getting remarried. I was so happy God had answered my prayers.

We had come to know a dear family, the Jacks. This couple especially became a big part of my family. They counselled my parents for quite some time. They led my parents to the Lord, and things were good for a time. My parents stayed married for twenty-two years the second time, but they sadly ended up divorced again.

Since my parents had asked Jesus into their hearts, they sat me down one day and asked, do you want to ask Jesus into your heart? Basically, I was told that if I didn't say this prayer that I would be going to hell. I ended up saying I would, but I was so angry, and I felt forced. I remember mumbling under my breath, 'I don't want to do this'; I did not mean what I prayed. It was done under pressure.

I also was baptised in that same church at age nine but honestly didn't really understand what I was doing. My brother and sister also were baptised. I remember been given the verses from Proverbs 3:5–6, 'Trust in the Lord with all your heart and do not lean on your own understanding; in all your ways acknowledge him, and he will make your paths straight.'

My life seemed stable for a couple of years. When my parents were married for the second time, that was probably one of the best times for me. We were involved in the church a fair bit. The church had a real heart for evangelising. I think the seed was planted in my heart then that I had a passion for sharing Jesus with other people. I used to go doorknocking with my pastor to tell people about God. I know I use to tell other kids at school about God. I was so passionate about it, even at a young age.

My siblings and I went to a different primary school, where I experienced some difficult times. First, my mum gave me a haircut that looked was so short and closely cropped that I looked like a boy, which didn't give me much self-esteem. With my parents not having much money, I remember being put in this atrocious-looking dress with clobber-hobber shoes from the dinosaur age. I was not a popular child. The teacher would walk around the playground and watch whether you were playing with other children. If you weren't, they would put you with whomever they wanted. The teacher would then leave, and the teasing would start. I would never be picked for games. I was the last one chosen for team sports. The rejection was painful. I ended up hiding from the teachers after that because there was nothing worse than being put with other kids who never wanted to be with you. I remember hiding under a school bench one time and crying my heart out, really hoping teachers wouldn't see me curled up in a ball trying to hide.

I could see cracks starting to appear in my parents' marriage. There were arguments and a lot of tension. My dad was drinking again, and things were starting to fall apart. My parents moved us to a different school, which was one of the worst things that ended up happening. We moved houses once again. Everything was unsettled. I hated school so much I used to run away and hide, so I didn't have to go. I used to say I was sick all the time so I could get out of going. The issues had gotten so bad my parents made the decision to put us back in our old school.

As things got worse with my parents, I remember being involved in an argument where they were literally pulling on one arm each. This again tore my heart in two. No child wants to pick sides between their parents.

I never got a belting from my dad except for one time. It was because I didn't want to play with our Labrador Retriever puppy. He was crazy and boisterous and full of energy and scared me. My dad had never known about a time when I was younger that I had been attacked by a dog. It had knocked me over and clawed my back. Yet, I got a belting for not playing with a dog, of which I was petrified.

The person I received my beltings from was my mum. She had some crazy ways of dealing with me. I felt physically abused by my mum. The beltings were usually done out of anger, even if she thought she was doing the right thing. She, at times, used to use what I would call a switch. They were thin, green, flexible branches or trees. She used to hit me across my legs, which would leave a scar. Another way she abused me was to rip my hair out and slap my face. Out of anger and to annoy her, I would slap the other side. That would drive her crazy, which is why I did it. My thought was, I can slap myself harder than you can. I think because of the abuse my mum had experienced her whole life, she took out her pain on my siblings and me.

My parents decided to move to a caravan park. We lived in a caravan that had two bedrooms in it. There were four bunks on one end, and my parents the other end with my baby brother on a portable cot. I remember having a shelf on my top bunk in which I placed all my dolls. It meant a lot to me. Even though my bed was tiny, to be able to have all my dolls on my bed was a big deal. Others may not understand this, but for a few months, my sister and I lived in a three-man tent. I thought it was heaven. We got to have just two children in what felt like it was a separate bedroom. The other little special touch for me at the time was that I got to make a dressing table out of a cardboard box. I put a tablecloth on it and thought it was the most beautiful thing I'd ever seen.

We upgraded our living facilities to what we called the tin shed. Pretty much a caravan with a big tin shed on the side. We had no toilet. We used to have to run about half a kilometre to the toilet block in the caravan park in rain, hail or shine. I remember one night it was pouring rain, and I had run to the toilet block, but I didn't make it. I can laugh now as I recall it, thinking of the things I went through growing up.

My mum and dad eventually bought that mobile home, which for them was the first place they had owned. I spent my teenage life there, and that was a whole other journey.

••• 3 •••

Who Am I? My Identity

After my parents moved into the mobile home, they decided to keep us in the same school. I was in my first year of high school. I enjoyed it, and I loved my teachers. Many teachers used to favour me. My grades were As. My test marks were Es (the lowest mark before fail), but the teachers seemed to ignore this and still gave me As. Being a teacher's pet came with a price. I was labelled a goody-two-shoes as well as a teacher's pet. It didn't bother me to start with, as it felt good having teachers on my side, but after some time, the teasing and not having friends started to break me. I felt lonely.

I got through my first year of high school and started year eight. One day my family decided to go on a trip to a relative's place. It was raining, and the roads were slippery. In a split second, we were in a car accident. I remember during the middle of the collision, it felt like it went on forever. It was in slow motion. I remember thinking, *Is this going to end?*

14

I looked up and saw a bus with people on it. The bus driver chose to stop to see if he could help. I was sitting in the middle of the back seat. The front end of the car was smashed in. Our car had turned and hit a car in oncoming traffic on the other side of the road. The front windscreen had smashed in and sprayed glass over my mum and my younger brother, who were both sitting in the front passenger's side. My brother was sitting on my mum's knee because back then, seatbelts weren't compulsory.

Everyone had been injured in some form or another, and I remember holding my neck. It was aching pretty bad. We were all taken to a hospital in Boxhill. My mum and brother had glass shards in their eyes. My brother and sister had injuries to themselves. I had whiplash, and my recovery was a very long journey that took years. They placed a brace on my neck, and that became who I was for a long time—the girl in a neck brace. The pain I felt the night of the car accident was so intense I could barely move. I had pillows stacked up all around me just to keep me still. I ended up taking a lot of time off school due to the injury. When I went back to school, things seemed OK for a while, but as months went on, I was getting teased, and it made it really hard to go each day. I would make excuses not to attend because I hated being teased for wearing my neck brace.

When I was attending school, I couldn't cope with not having friends, so I started getting desperate in wanting them. I started choosing friends who were bad influences. They were the 'in-crowd' at the time. They smoked cigarettes had wild parties. They always seemed to be in trouble with the teachers. I started doing things like them, so I would get their attention like getting in trouble with teachers and vandalising school property. I helped some boys light a fire in a school classroom through a power switch. I would smash and hide the school clocks. In my mind and heart, I was hurting, and I tried to do anything I could to get attention.

At the time, things seemed worse at home too. There was more tension and arguments between my parents. I was feeling depressed after the car accident and the whiplash. I also had representatives from the insurance companies watching my every move. They were men employed to watch people who had been involved in car accidents to see if the injured person was telling the truth, which had me feeling unsettled. I felt like they were trying to make me feel as if my injury was all a lie because of how they were watching me. They took notes on my every move from the moment I stepped out of my front door; they were watching me. I started seeing a counsellor at school, but it didn't seem to help, and out of desperation to the mental pain I was going through in my mind, I started cutting my wrists. I hid it from everyone. Neither anyone at school nor my parents knew. I used to do it because I felt so unloved and rejected. It felt like I was punishing myself. I went from an A student to an E student rather fast. From that time on, my grades never picked up again, and I was always at the bottom end of the grading. Exams were a very stressful time. I barely passed any of them.

Growing up, I always had eating issues, which tend to make me feel like using food as a source of comfort, and therefore, as a teenager, I overate. Food became a convenience to ease my mind of bad thoughts in times of pain. My mum would make comments about how I was eating too much, which made me feel worse. I would eat more food to try to make myself feel better. I was chubby in my younger teenage life. I had no self-esteem. I didn't get much encouragement at home, which made me feel invisible, and I longed to be seen and heard just by someone.

One day I overheard a conversation between my parents. My dad said to my mum, 'You need to have the talk with her.' This talk was about girls getting their periods. When she told me, I was totally devastated and in shock that such a thing was going to happen to my body for many years to come. I did not want to embrace becoming a woman. I wanted to run from it. To me, it felt dirty. I remember feeling so glad the talk was over. But my mum made a song and dance out of it. She told my sister and aunty we had the talk, and it was like they were having a party for me. On the inside, I was dying. I wanted to run to the mountains and never return. I never wanted to hear about it or talk about it ever again!

About three weeks after that talk, I joined the womanhood club and was told only the basics—that this new 'friend' would visit once a month and that I would have to use these things called pads when the visit came. I was also told a lie that when this monthly friend came visiting, I was not in any way allowed to have a shower or wash my hair, and I'd pretty much die if I did. I found out a few years later, it was an old wives' tale. As far as I know today, it came from a time in my Nanna's generation, so she didn't have to cart water a long way during her time of the month.

That lie made me even more devastated about getting my period. Seriously, I stank! My smell and greasy hair were embarrassing. I might as well have had leprosy. My sister and I would get so desperate we would sneak and wash our hair. One time. I washed my hair, and my mum yelled, 'Are you washing your hair?'

I grabbed a towel and went like a crazy lady rubbing it as hard as I could to dry it. Then my mum called out, 'Come here and let me see!'

So, I walked into her room, looking like I had stuck my finger in an electrical outlet. I looked at her and said, 'No, I haven't washed my hair.' It was hilarious in a way, but deep-down crippling for a young girl.

I had a chance to attend a few youth camps from about age fourteen to sixteen. It was one of these camps where the most amazing thing ever happened in my life. It was when I allowed true love to enter my heart. We were down in a valley. It was a beautiful sunrise, and it was Easter Sunday. I decided finally of my own free will to ask Jesus to come into my heart and be my true love and Lord of my life. I sat on a log with one of the youth leaders and asked Jesus into my heart. I had the vertical vision of a wooden cross in front of me. I remember being on my knees in the long grass afterward and feeling overwhelmed with joy. I had received my first kiss, spiritually. I was in awe. This time no one had forced me, unlike when I was eight years old and was forced to say a prayer to ask Jesus into my heart. Now, I embraced the lover of my soul from my own free will. There is nothing really that can compare in this world. Love entered, chose me, pursued me, and finally held me in an embrace that was eternity-bound. I knew I'd decided to choose Jesus, but making him Lord in my life didn't happen for a while.

Except for a crush in I had in high school, this was when I started taking an interest in boys as in a relationship. My mum had been very strict on us dating. Her age set was sixteen. I started taking an interest in boys and they in me. I had my first encounter with a boy before I was sixteen. I never let my mum know about him. I used to get him to send letters to a girlfriend's place so my mum wouldn't find out, and I would sneak phone calls in when my mum wasn't around. I also would sneak and catch the bus to see him. I'd lie to my mum about where I was going. The relationship became too hard because I wasn't allowed to date yet. It fizzled out, but we stayed friends.

When I was close to turning sixteen, and I knew I was nearly at the age where my mum would allow me to start dating. I was counting the days. I was at another camp and officially started dating a guy I felt so proud to tell my mum about, but it lasted only a few days. I had my first heartbreak. He decided we lived too far away from each other and ended it. I found out later he was interested in another girl. That left me feeling rejected.

It got near the end of me being in year ten, and I had my heart set on finishing high school in another two years, but something happened that has held me in chains my whole life until only a few months ago. My parents decided to take me out of school. They said basically I was too dumb for school (not in those words). My grades were low, and my parents thought it was a waste of time and their money for me to finish school, so they made the decision I wasn't to finish school. They thought I would be better off working, and I was totally heartbroken as I went around to all my schoolteachers to tell them I was leaving. I felt humiliated, telling them the reason. I felt stripped of who I was and who I could have become. I never got a chance to say goodbye to my friends properly. I was just told I had to leave and get a job. From that event, I never felt I was good enough to do anything. I never had any ambitions. I chose to believe in the lie that I was too dumb for school.

I end up getting a job in a supermarket called Tuckerbag. It was my first full-time job. My mum was very strict with my pay. I was never allowed to spend them on what I wanted. Board had to be paid and money put aside for different things. I was not even allowed to buy lunches with my money. We barely ever had food at home, either. I used to scour the ground for loose change to buy a chocolate bar and a meat pie each day. I ended up using my pays to buy food for my family every week because I couldn't stand watching them go without. My mum let me do this.

It came time for another youth camp. During the last couple of years, I had dated a few different guys. I ended up dating a young guy from one of these camps who also attended my church youth group. I was warned not to date this guy by many friends, and my parents didn't like him. I found out the hard way. This guy had one thing on his mind, and it was sex. He was never in love with me. I found out later I was used as a rebound girl.

One night he was driving me back from the youth group, and he pulled the car over not far from my house. I thought it was strange. We kissed, which was normal, but then suddenly, things went further. I froze. He raped me. I was devastated.

I remember going into my house with tears streaming down my face. I wanted to ring the police. I wanted to tell my parents, but all these voices were screaming in my head, saying it was my fault, and I had no right to tell anyone what happened. That night I buried what happened so deep I would tell no one about it for a long time. It was the most debilitating thing. So many thoughts rushed through my head, but mostly I just remember being frozen. I wanted to shower but couldn't. I was scared, and I felt dirty and used. My head and heart raced like a tornado. At the time, I thought the best way to deal with it was to pretend it never happened, which is pretty much what I did.

After that happened, we broke up, and I started dating another guy. On the first date, I was already getting sexually abused. I started to think about what was wrong with me that I was getting treated that way. I started to believe I was not valuable. A repeat cycle was happening through my life of feeling unloved. I didn't feel loved by my parents or my friends. It was a horrible place to be. The trouble was I started believing I had become unlovable.

One particular day our company had decided to go on strike due to union matters. So, a party was organised at one of my co-worker's houses. I was asked if I wanted a drink. I never had drunk alcohol before, so I said I'd have one, but it was really strong and went straight to my head. I was told by the storeman (in charge of all the stock in the store) at the time that I should go and put water on my face in the bathroom. He followed me in there, and in the next minute, he was trying to rape me.

I felt so scared. I ran outside to the front lawn crying and ended up ringing a friend to pick me up. I didn't want to go home because I had been drinking, and I knew my parents would be so angry with me, so I ran away. The friend who picked me up said I couldn't stay with him, so I asked if he could drop me at my workplace. I thought I would just sleep in the staff room, but the night shift crew said it was against regulations to let me in.

It was a really cold night, and all I had was a big, pink handbag and a coat. I had nowhere to go, so I found a tree or more like a bush and curled up under it. Shortly after, a young boy from my work rode past on his bike and said, 'You can't stay here. You will get raped or something.'

So, I went back to his house and slept in the back garden shed. I was so exhausted from all the issues that I fell asleep on a mattress on the shed floor, cold and feeling alone. The next morning, I walked back to work to deal with the police and people in my workplace. Apparently, I was reported missing by my family. I know they would have been concerned for me. I turned up home that night, and my mum was very angry about me running away from home and not telling her or anyone else in my family where I was. She belted me, slapped my face, and ripped my hair out. All I wanted was to feel loved and wanted. I was naïve and didn't really understand how so little alcohol could affect so easily. Since I had seen my dad drink, I knew alcohol was bad if too much was consumed, but I had never had alcohol until that day and felt its effects for myself.

I was taken advantage of by other men at work, even married men. I had been offered a modelling job while I had been at this supermarket. I went to start getting my portfolio together. I'd had all the photos done, but I never felt comfortable doing it. I went home to show my mum my photos and tell her I had made the decision not to do modelling. But before I got the chance, she threw my photos in the air and started belting me again, ripping my hair out and slapping me. I let her do this and waited for her to calm down. Then

I looked at her and said, 'I decided before you had belted me that I wasn't going to do modelling.' The look on her face was one who was utterly stunned.

I continued to work where I was but started to show symptoms of becoming very sick.

••• 4 •••

When Pain Strikes

I met my future husband, Wes, when I was around age sixteen. We are still together today. I was at a convention in Belgrave Heights, and I was dating another guy at the time. I was standing at the side of the auditorium, and I saw a friend I knew on the other side. Before I could go up to this friend and say hello, I noticed another guy standing with my friend. I heard a voice in my head saying, 'You are going to marry that guy one day.'

I thought I was going crazy. *Did I just hear a voice say I am going to marry a guy I don't even know?* I laughed to myself in disbelief. I was content with the guy I was dating and passed the thought off as nothing.

As things turned out, the other guy—my now-husband— worked about five shops away from where I did. He turned up at my work, and he remembered we had been introduced to each other at the convention. I was working on the cash registers. He was standing in a queue with two people in front of him with two great big trolleys full of groceries.

I looked up at him and said, 'There is an express lane you can go through.'

He looked at me with a smile and his couple of items and said, 'I don't mind waiting.'

I laughed to myself and thought, *This guy is keen on me if he is willing to wait all that time just so I can serve him.*

He started coming into the store regularly. By that time, I wasn't dating anyone, and he asked me out on a date with his youth group to go roller skating. I could not roller skate for peanuts! I had to have one person on either side of me to hold my hands as I attempted to skate. I sat down beside my future husband, and he did the sly trick of slipping his arm around my shoulder. Later that night, he asked me to be his girlfriend, and I accepted.

I think the memory of the thought that I would marry him one day made me believe it was going to happen. We had only been dating for a couple of months, but we knew we wanted to be with each other and get married. We were attending the Royal Melbourne Show, and I wasn't feeling well. I fainted and ended up in the ambulance tent. I was laying on one of the beds, ambulance officers were checking over me, and I was in a bit of a daze. I looked up and could see Wes was standing near me.

He looked at me, concern etched on his face, and said, 'I am going to marry you one day.' That was my official proposal!

After spending some time with each other and getting to know one another, we soon realised we lived close to each other. Wes lived on a farm which pretty much backed onto the caravan park I was living in at the time.

I continued working at the supermarket for a while, but I began having some health issues. I started getting pain in my stomach. I started losing my appetite. I started having to take time off work due to my pain levels increasing. When I was working, I was doubled over in pain. I would pretend to drop something on the ground just so I could hold my stomach. If I wasn't working on the cash register, I was out in the back doing stock, but the pain was so debilitating that I would hide out in the storeroom amongst the pellets where no one could find me.

I went to doctors, but no one could find out what was wrong with me. I had people and doctors telling me the pain was in my head. I tried to convince myself that the physical sensations I was feeling were all in my head. I can barely put in words what that did to me mentally. The pain was real, but no one would believe me. People started to think I had mental issues and talked about me going to see a psychologist. It wasn't long, though, before I got so sick and had lost so much weight that I was rushed to the former Fairfield Infectious Diseases Hospital in Melbourne.

I was so weak I could barely walk. I was stuck in a bathroom in such a bad state I couldn't get to the buzzer to call a nurse. I just lay there and cried until eventually, someone came to check me. My body looked like a skeleton. My eyes had sunken in. I thought I was going to die, and so did others. After a week of tests in the hospital, no one was any wiser about what was wrong with me. I was sent home and given a referral to see a specialist. I saw the specialist, and he said he thought I had anorexia. Again, my physical pain was dismissed. I was angry, wondering why no one would believe me. The trouble was that everyone else started believing I had anorexia, as well.

I felt so alone and rejected. Not even the doctors believed me that something was wrong. I was given a referral to get a colonoscopy done, but I considered that the last resort. One of the physical symptoms I had was diarrhoea. Any food I ate went straight through me. I remember being so weak one time that I was covered in a mess from the diarrhoea. My mum and dad had to carry me to the shower. I felt so humiliated. I'd lost my dignity. I had become a bag of bones. The only thing I could tolerate was milk.

I finally decided to get the colonoscopy done. They discovered I had Crohn's disease. After everything I'd been through, I was relieved they found out what was wrong with me, but at the same time, I was angry with all the people who had not believed something bad was wrong with me. Psychologically, that did horrible things to me. The fact that no one would believe me made me angry and frustrated. As crazy as it sounds, I wanted those people to live inside my body for five minutes to experience my pain so they would understand and know that what I was sharing with them was real. Finally, I knew what was wrong, and it was the start of a journey that lasted for a few years of my life.

Wes knew about my Crohn's disease, and I thought it would put him off of wanting to marry me, but it didn't. We had planned to get married after two months, but we knew our parents would have struggled with that, so we decided to wait another three months. Then Wes asked my parents if he could marry me. They said yes. My dad made a joke about it being one less mouth to feed. Things at home were not in a good way. I was using my paycheck each week to provide my family with food. There was barely ever proper food. So, for me, getting married meant that I'd have the security I had never really experienced before. Wes' parents were concerned we were too young, as I was only seventeen, and Wes was twenty. They still gave consent, though, and we announced our engagement on Christmas Day 1988.

I was in and out of the hospital right up until our wedding. I worked on our plans for our wedding from my hospital bed. I was determined to get married on the date we set, even to the point I told the doctors, 'I'm going down the aisle even if I am in a wheelchair.' The doctors put me on a medication called prednisolone, which had so many side effects that caused my body a lot of damage. One of the major side effects was a massive weight gain. My body literally blew up like a balloon. I had bad stretch marks as a result. The disease brought excruciating pain and stopped me from physically being able to walk around.

No one understood how much pain I was in. I noticed after some time people got sick of me telling them I was in pain. The pain was written all over my face. I ended up leaving work, and I never returned. Wes knew this, but again still chose to stay with me. It got to the point that other people hated being around me. I was called many names, and unfortunately, I believed what people said about me. I remember, at one time, being torn down verbally by someone, and I became so angry that I thought to myself, *If you could feel my pain just for one minute, you would understand what my life was really like.*

The disease seemed to be getting worse with time, but I was still determined to walk down the aisle with Wes no matter what.

••• 5 •••

The Honeymoon Period

There were many preparations leading up to the day of our wedding. I made a lot of small details myself while I was sick at home. The bridesmaids' flowers, the name seat tags, flowers to hang down the aisle in the church, and many other things. My parents and Wes' parents had different ideas from one another. My parents didn't want alcohol or dancing. This broke my heart more than anyone will ever know. My parents said if we had dancing, they would not attend our wedding. Wes' parents loved dancing, but we felt we had to oblige my parents. We were not even allowed a wedding waltz with each other.

We had four bridesmaids and four groomsmen in our wedding party. Since my parents didn't have money, it was a big deal to get the funds to help pay for it. My parents had to take out a loan from the bank for $1,500 to pay for the reception. After all the planning, the day finally arrived. We were married at the Dandenong Uniting Church in Dandenong on the 2nd of September 1989, at 2:30 in the afternoon. We had over two hundred people attend. Bagpipes played as I walked down the aisle. All the planning and the day had finally arrived. We had a big afternoon tea and our reception at a hall in Belgrave Heights.

Like many other couples getting married for the first time, something we longed for was to have beautiful photos of the day. We decided to have our wedding photos done at Sherbrooke Forest in The Dandenongs. With the beautiful backdrop of Australian gum trees, we thought the photos would have been magical. But when we eventually got the wedding photos back, all the photos had been blacked out. There were no trees in the photos. It was just black backgrounds. I was devastated. Was it a joke? It was real. Somehow the photographer had messed up, and we had no wedding photos. The only thing we were able to do was to ask people who had attended the wedding what snapshots they had taken and asked if we could have any photos anyone had. It felt like a bad omen not having these photos.

At the end of the wedding day, I was sort of scared of what to expect with the wedding night. I was a pretty naïve young girl in the sense of not really understanding what was expected of me on the first night. No one had talked to me about the birds and the bees. Because of not knowing about this, it became the most painful night of my life to that point. This set a picture in my head for a long time that sex was the most horrible thing in life.

I wanted to share about this because back in my early days and my parents' time and grandparents' time, sex was never to be talked about and even came across as something dirty. God created sex as a gift and a form of intimacy between a husband and a wife to make a union between the two. The two shall become one flesh! In my mind, we should make it our responsibility to teach our children the right way about sex.

It's not something that should be hidden under the carpet. God created it. In the Song of Solomon, it goes into detail how beautiful sex really is when done in a blessed marriage.

My view of sex scarred me for twelve years after Wes and I were married. It became more of a duty than an act of love. There was no pleasure in it. I could have gone to the doctor and talked to them, but I was taught you didn't talk about sex, so I accepted it. My view was so wrong in every way, and if I can help someone else not to go through this, then my book has been worth it.

We went on our honeymoon for a couple of weeks travelling around Victoria in our caravan. Then, after two weeks of married life, reality set in. Wes had to get back into the farm work pretty much straight away. I never had my driver's licence, so I became reliant on Wes and his parents to take me shopping or get anywhere. We were living on the farm where Wes had lived his whole life. I didn't really know anything about farming but learnt the realities of it quickly. On the farm, you learnt about life and death. It was part of life every day there. I remember my first experience of death was of some baby birds on our roof in the mobile home we were living in. They had made a nest, and it was blocking the drains. If humans touch baby birds, the parents wouldn't want to feed them, so those baby birds had to be killed. I cried. Being on a farm was real. It came with many challenges over the years while I was there.

As time went on, my Crohn's disease got worse. The pain was incredible. I had put so much weight on that I looked like a different person. The amount of food I ate was crazy. I just remember always feeling hungry, even during the night. The prednisone had increased my appetite in a big way. I had gone from being this girl who was like a bag of bones to a girl who was blown up like a balloon.

I didn't seem to be improving on the medication I was on, as my pain was increasing. I had been on some herbal medication from a naturopath and was told it would heal me. I was on it for a couple of years. I had put trust in this naturopath and thought her treatment would work, but it didn't. The pain was getting so bad I decided to have yet another colonoscopy done. The doctors discovered the Crohn's disease had spread to both my small intestine and the large intestine where the two meet. I was only twenty-one years old. I had to decide what I wanted to do with my life.

One of the options was the prednisone medication that had really bad side effects. The other option my doctor presented was to have an operation to remove the part of the bowel that was affected by the disease. In my current state, I wasn't able to enjoy life anymore, so I made the decision to get a portion of both of my bowels removed.

I went into the hospital, not really knowing what my outcome would be. I actually thought I was going to die. There was no promise that getting this part of my bowels removed would be a permanent fix to my disease. It felt risky, but I couldn't cope with the pain. To try and describe the pain, I would say it was like someone walking around on the inside of your guts with a knife with no break in the pain. It was always there. There was nothing you could physically take to even ease the pain. To walk was painful. The only thing that gave me a small amount of comfort was holding a wheat pack on my stomach.

As I was wheeled into the operating theatre, I thought, *I may not come out of this alive*. I didn't feel I had a deep peace with God either. The operation took many hours, and I did not know what to expect when I awoke. The pain was incredible, even being on an anaesthetic. I remember being slid on a slippery board from operating bed to a bed in the hospital ward. I had tubes and wires coming out of me everywhere. I was surprised how quickly they seem to want to get you moving, especially after such a major operation.

I lay in my hospital bed feeling angry, wondering if others knew the pain I was in. I wasn't allowed to eat for days after the operation. There was one tube in my lower abdomen that was so painful. Every time I moved, it felt like my guts were being ripped out. It felt like my life was going from one painful event to the next. Looking out the window of my hospital bed, I had thoughts about my relationship with God. I wondered where God was in all of this. I had had this disease for six years by then. I thought to myself, *Why would God let me go through this? Why would God let me feel such pain? Why would God let people hate me just because I was in pain?* Nothing seemed fair. I didn't really feel close to God. I believed in Him. I went to church, but where was He?

It took some time to heal. Eventually, my body did, but there would always be a scar—a scar to remember this painful time in my life. The way I had been sewn back up made me look deformed. I no longer had a flat stomach but a ridge that would be there until I left my physical body to go home to heaven one day. It left a mark in my mind that I was no longer good enough.

I felt like I lived on the edge for many years after that. I don't know if I really got over it. Every time I have pain in my stomach, the memory lingers. Is that Crohn's disease coming back? For many years, it was always the thing doctors would say was wrong with me. My life did go back to normal, something I had not experienced in six years—not to have pain, to walk again, not doubled over, to enjoy life again, to have a smile on my face again. I had lost my smile and the will to live. The surgery gave me a second chance at life.

During that time, Wes and I experienced marriage problems. After the first year, it looked like things were going to fall apart. We had a lot to learn, as we were still very young. We didn't know how to communicate well. We decided we needed help in our marriage and found a counsellor to seek advice to strengthen our marriage, where issues were surfacing and needed attention. It helped for a while in practical ways, but as I look back now, I see that heart change in either one of us never happened. It was like putting on a bandage, which only masked far greater issues that arose later.

••• 6 •••

Jesus Took My Baby Home

We had been married for five years, and the idea of having children had come around. I think when you first talk about having children, it's a bit of shock I must admit I had a lot of fear there. With everything that had happened to me with Crohn's disease, I thought I would never be able to have children.

I prayed to God, *Please just let me get pregnant, even if you take the baby home.* I can honestly say it was a prayer, the depth of which I did not recognise. It was always in the back of my mind, but when I prayed this prayer, it wasn't in any way meant for that to happen. All I wanted from God was to know I could get pregnant. I was hoping God got that message. It was a half-hearted prayer with no intention of really wanting what I prayed.

The first month came, and I waited with anticipation. The waiting was hard, and it was only the first month of trying, but there was no success. I probably coped alright with that, but fear was whispering loudly that I could not have children. The next month came, and again there were no results—stress set in already. Fear had taken over me, even though it was only the second month of trying. One day when you are trying to have a baby feels like a month. It came to the third month of trying, and it had finally happened. I know three months isn't a long time compared to what other women who are trying to have children go through. I think after six years of being sick, I had lost hope in many things—even wanting to live at times—because of the pain.

I took the pregnancy test and felt shocked. I think Wes was too. I mean, it's one thing to say you want to try to have a baby, and another when it really happens. So, we went off to the doctors to get a blood test done, and it was confirmed. We were having a baby! I felt excited about being pregnant.

I had decided to keep a diary for the pregnancy, and when I wrote this book, I felt God wanted me to look at once again. None of this book was easy to write. When I came to areas that waved a red flag, I thought, *I don't want to go back to that memory.* But with each bad memory, God came alongside me and held my hand.

I opened my diary recently, and only a couple of pages in I saw the sentence, 'I am writing this diary so one day you can read about how you became a little human being.' Tears flooded my eyes. The memories felt like they were only yesterday, but it's been twenty-four years since I held my first baby in my arms.

I was very enthusiastic about getting things to set up the nursery—actually too excited, some people said. We had bought nearly everything we needed, leaving others with no ideas what to get. I loved knitting and sewing things for the baby. I was getting morning sickness for the first few months.

The 14th of December 1994 was the first time we saw him—ten little fingers and ten little toes, and we heard his heartbeat. He was perfect. It looked like he was waving at us. He wasn't cooperating very well on getting the scan done. The date we were given for him to be born was the 18th of May 1995.

It was February 1995, and I had packed his hospital bag. I was a bit eager, as I was only twenty-three weeks along. I had a little kitten named Monty for a few months that I had reared from two days old. I had attached myself to him and bottle-fed him. I found out he had been killed on the road, and I was devastated. I felt angry, wondering why God took him. Now in a funny way, I look back and think that losing my kitten was preparing me for what was ahead.

We had been to church one Sunday and came home to a shock. Wes' mum had left his dad, and we could not contact her. She left us with a note saying she had gone. I remember feeling stressed. We had planned to go away that following weekend with my parents to South Australia to a wedding. I really wanted to go away, but while something inside me was saying not to go, I refused to listen.

All through my pregnancy, I had pain. The doctor always said it was due to my Crohn's disease. We got up early to leave, and I had this really bad pain inside me. I remember sitting on the step of the mobile home where we were living, and the pain was incredible. I got a heated pack and put it on my stomach to help ease the pain. I can't deny here the thought of something being wrong with my baby had entered my head, but I was determined it would go away.

It ended up being one of the hottest weekends in years. I was at the reception and drinking lemonade, which always used to make my baby do summersaults inside me, but I didn't feel him move. On our drive home, I had really bad swelling in my ankles. I could barely walk. We eventually got home, and I started feeling stressed that, even after drinking the lemonade, I hadn't felt him move for days. I told Wes I just wanted to go to the doctor and hear the baby's heartbeat. That night I had also had a dream that my baby had died.

So, we went to the doctor, and he put the hand-held implement on my tummy but couldn't hear anything. Then he put the battery-operated one on and still couldn't hear it. He didn't seem concerned that he couldn't hear the heartbeat, but he did give a form to go to the hospital to get an ultrasound done. We went there, and they said we couldn't get an appointment for three weeks.

I was getting really upset. I just wanted to hear my baby's heartbeat, so I said to Wes, 'Let's just walk down to the maternity section of the hospital and speak to them.' We walked in and told them we just wanted to hear our baby's heartbeat as it had been days since I felt him move. The nurse first treated me like an overly worried mother. She nearly wasn't going to do anything. I felt embarrassed that I even asked, but I was persistent and wanted to hear his heartbeat.

I was taken to a bed, and they used a portable hand-held ultrasound device, but the nurse couldn't hear anything. So, they got the battery-operated implement out and still couldn't hear the heartbeat. It wasn't long, and I was being wheeled off in a wheelchair to get an ultrasound. I didn't think anything was wrong except he was in a bad position, and no one could hear him properly.

The doctor did the ultrasound and said nothing to me. He brought in another doctor, but no words were spoken. There were just hand actions between the two doctors. I was wheeled back down a long hallway that seemed to go forever. The nurse was quiet, not saying anything.

I got back to the room and hopped onto the bed. The doctor walked in, looked at me quite casually, I thought, and said, 'I'm sorry, but we can't pick up the foetal heartbeat.'

I replied, 'So what can you do?'

He looked at me and said straight out, 'Your baby has died'.

Of course, I didn't believe the doctor. I kept asking what they could do to help my baby. I was in denial and shock at what had just been said to me. I was walking up and down the corridors crying, and all of a sudden, I remembered my prayer I first prayed to God, *Please just let me get pregnant even if you take my baby.* Today, I understand that God never causes evil, but He uses the bad things that happen in our lives to bring good. I had blamed God for my kitten dying because, at this time in my life, I had so many misconceptions of God. That's what I automatically did. When it came to my baby, I never blamed God.

It felt like no time was allowed for us to take in what was just said to me, and all of a sudden, in the reality of the situation, decisions had to be made. I was extremely naïve, as this was my first baby. They asked how I wanted to have the baby. I felt like it was a joke because the reality of his death had not set in yet. I said, 'Can't you just take him out?' They said I would have to go through labour.

I asked about a caesarean, but they said because it was my first child, it probably wasn't a good idea. The only other option was normal childbirth. It seemed cruel, though. I thought, *Why should I go through labour and get nothing but more pain out of it?* My mind was obviously not thinking properly in any matter. I was in so much shock I could barely think. Basically, this was what I was hit with: 'You must go into labour and deliver your dead baby. Your breast milk will come in, but you obviously won't have a baby drinking off you, so you'll need to take medication to dry up your milk.'

I was then told that because he was over twenty weeks, a funeral would need to be arranged. That included organising a cemetery, a coffin, and a church service. It was hugely overwhelming. The nurse said I could go home for the night just to get my head around all that had just happened. She gave me sleeping tablets to take when I got home. Wes and I had rung some close friends and told them about our baby. They came over to be with us and comfort us.

I wanted to have a shower. In the shower, I don't know what happened, but all of a sudden, I felt disgusted with myself. All I could think about was, *Get this dead thing out of me.* By the dates of the ultrasound I was given, my baby had been dead inside me for nearly two weeks. When they gave me the dates, I pinpointed it to the day I was sitting on the steps of the mobile home before we went away. The thought of a dead human inside me was making me sick. I was crying and nearly screaming. I took the sleeping tablets with our visitors still in our place, comforting Wes.

I finally laid my head on my pillow and slept amazingly until around 6 a.m. the next day. I saw the sunrise, and I can't explain it except to say God had his hand on me. I was peaceful, calm, and had a clear mind to think. I sat at the table and sorted all my bills out, and I even wrote out a card to give to some friends. Everything that needed to be done was before I went into the hospital.

We left to go to the hospital, and I remember walking down what felt like a dark, eerie hallway. I walked to the nurses' desk and registered. They took me to my room, and as I walked in, one of the most incredibly painful things happened. I heard the most crippling sound: a lady in labour in the next room. She had just given birth, and I heard her baby cry. I looked at the nurses and at Wes, and a scream of a cry came out with words, 'My baby is not going to cry when he comes out!' From that moment on, tears flooded for weeks, barely stopping.

I was asked then what decision I had made on how I was going to give birth. I decided to have an epidural because I didn't want to feel the pain of childbirth with nothing in my hands to hold onto at the end. They induced me to begin what ended up being twenty-six-hour labour. It was one of the hottest days on record, too.

I had asked both my mum and Wes' mum to be in the room with us. My family doctor at the time, Doctor Beech, came in just to see me out of his own time. My gynaecologist also came in numerous times, which touched my heart. My labour wasn't progressing. I found out he was breech.

Saturday had passed, and Sunday had come. There was still no sign of him wanting to come out. They broke my waters. The hard part started. I had to push a breech baby out, I was told. I had already been in labour for nearly a whole day. I did have the epidural, but it didn't seem to be doing a lot to dull the pain. I think I spent an hour pushing, and finally, his little bottom came out, and the nurse pulled his little feet out and then his arms. I was exhausted. I had no strength left. His head was bigger than his bottom, and I had to find something deep inside me to push his head out. It took about an hour of pushing. Finally, he came out.

They handed him to me, and I looked at him. He was warm. I looked into his eyes and was oblivious to everything. He was still warm. I mean, all he had to do was take a breath. I held him and said, 'Breathe, little one. Just breathe.' Right up to the last second, I hoped he would be alive. I wanted him to be.

He was perfect. He had ten little fingers and ten little toes. He had a whole head of hair too, which I thought was amazing for twenty-six weeks old. Here was this beautiful little boy, warm but not alive. The nurses asked if I wanted him dressed in a gown that was provided by the hospital. It was beautiful: white and hand-knitted by some volunteers at the hospital. We put him in a little blue bonnet and wrapped him in a blanket.

We made phone calls and told all our relatives they could come to see their grandson, nephew, and cousin because this would be all they would see of him. It felt a busy time with many friends and relatives showing love.

I was approached by the nurses and asked if I wanted to do an autopsy. Initially, I didn't know what they meant. Then they told me. They basically said we want to cut him up and see why he died. I was devasted and angry—as if I hadn't been through enough.

We were given the opportunity to spend the night with him in the hospital. Wes and me and our baby, for whom we'd chosen the name James Wesley Brough, stayed together for one night. James was born on Sunday, the 26th of February 1995, at 12:26 p.m. They put him in this beautiful bassinet, and we slept with him overnight. We had to decide about having an autopsy by the morning.

I woke up, and I could smell a smell I won't forget. It was the smell of death in our room. It came from James' body. Not a nice smell. We decided to go through with the autopsy because we wanted more children. I found it really hard, and it was also going to be our last physical goodbye because they said once they cut him up, he would not really look presentable. My heart continually was being broken, with each painstaking step of losing him.

I went home with empty arms—no baby to hold. I walked into his nursery all set up and just cried and cried in pain, disbelief, and shock. It felt like I was living in a whirlwind that wasn't going to stop. The next day came, and I had thought I had a blood clot, so we rushed back to the hospital to the emergency department and something I wasn't expecting happened.

For some reason, I was known all over the hospital. Everybody knew my baby had died. I heard so many stories of how my little baby's death had affected so many lives. I was told how the staff all over the hospital had gone off and cried away from me. This wasn't an unusual event. Other women had lost babies, but for some reason, my baby touched lives and hearts like no one else before. It turned out I didn't have a blood clot. I wondered if me going back in there was God showing me that James' little life mattered.

We went home, and the next day we had the funeral director come over to arrange James' funeral. I was crying most of the time. I could barely think of going through all the process of organising his funeral. An order of service had to be made and songs picked. The songs were 'All to Jesus', 'I Surrender', and 'Jesus Loves Me'. All I could think about was James being held in Jesus' arms, so the song 'Jesus Loves Me' felt so appropriate.

A couple of days later, the day of the funeral was one of the hardest days of my life—burying my son. We had the service for James at the church where I got up and shared my heart about the seven months I had him inside me. I know on this day it was only God who carried me through. There was an afternoon tea provided by church people for everyone at the church. A dear friend I called Mr. Jack took the church service. He had been involved in my life since I was eight years old. A poem called 'The Master Weaver' was read. It talked about how we don't see the finished picture, but God does. In our human comprehension, we cannot understand God's whole picture for all of eternity, but thank goodness He does.

After the church service, we were driven in a white car with James' coffin. We got out of the car, and Wes carried the coffin over to the graveside, where all our friends and family were waiting. We had decided to bury James with Wes' grandparents as it saved a lot of money. Watching the coffin being lowered into the ground was heartbreaking. I had put a little teddy in with him. I think it comforted me in a crazy way that he had the teddy with him. I remember staring down at the coffin, lost and broken, and saying my last goodbye. I remember asking Jesus to please give James a big hug. I dropped a rose onto his coffin and said, 'Goodbye, my darling until I see you in heaven.'

••• 7 •••

Four Blessings
After the Storm

After James died, I felt lost in many ways. I didn't really feel supported in the church I was in and was craving something to fill an emptiness I was feeling. My parents were attending a church, and they asked if we wanted to go there. We did, and they seemed very caring for quite a while, so it was this church at which Wes and I decided to stay at for many years.

Many thoughts ran through my mind after losing my baby. *Could I have any more children? Did I want any more children? What if it happened again?* After James died, there were friends and relatives around us for about two weeks, but then it died down. I felt all alone and isolated. I thought to myself, *where did everyone go? Didn't people understand I was still grieving?*

Wes and I thought maybe we just needed a holiday, time away to think about everything that had just happened. It ended up being the worst thing we could have done. We were alone when we should have reached out to friends about how much we were hurting. We went away to a beach place called Venus Bay, and it was quiet—too quiet. We were alone with our thoughts, and they weren't good. We both laid on a bed and talked about taking our lives. That's how incredible the pain was for both of us.

I wanted another child desperately, but all I could think was, *What if this happens again?* No words can really express how it feels to have lost your baby and not be able to hold him in your hands. Everywhere I went, I felt like every second woman was pregnant. There was something inside my heart that I felt I couldn't even try to have another baby until his birth due date was up on the 18th of May. In my heart, I felt like I needed to grieve, but at the same time, I longed to hold another baby. That was three months away from losing James at twenty-eight weeks. That three months seemed like it went on forever. It ended up taking another three months for me to get pregnant. To put into words how hard this was, it was like someone stabbing your heart each day. Empty wombs cry a deep pain that is hard to bear.

Six months after losing James, I was carrying another baby. The first twelve weeks of the pregnancy felt like walking on eggshells. I had a gynaecologist right from the start of my pregnancy because I was considered high-risk. I had bad morning sickness up until twenty weeks. I had a baby shower, and we also moved into Wes' grandparents' house from our little mobile home. I didn't really want to know the sex of the baby, so it was a surprise. The nursery was painted light pale green with white to suit either gender. I was scared when it came to the twenty-six-week mark of the pregnancy because that's when James had died. The memories came flooding back. I got through that time and got to thirty-seven weeks.

I was lying in bed one night, and all of a sudden, I felt like I had wet the bed. I rang my mum and asked her if she knew what was happening. She said, 'Your waters have broken, so you need to go to the hospital.' I had my hospital bag already packed and felt quite excited. The thought of finally having a child that was going to be alive in my hands and I would be able to hold thrilled me.

I walked in and laid on the bed, and the nurse took all my observations. Then within minutes, the whole situation changed. I was told my blood pressure was extremely high, and I had what they called preeclampsia. At first, I didn't really understand what it was, but when I saw fear in the nurses' eyes, and that was enough to start scaring me. The staff and doctors said I needed to have an IV put in, and I would have to have an epidural as that helped with the preeclampsia. It was a form of hypertension disorder that could take my life and the baby's. I could not believe this was happening. I was praying and begging God not to let this baby die too. Little did I know was how close I was to death. I was so concerned about the baby. Meanwhile, my body was shutting down.

I was put in an area of the maternity section for women who were having serious problems with labour. They induced me at a quick rate to try to get the baby out quickly. The baby wouldn't come out, though. The head was stuck; meanwhile, I was getting closer to death. They decided to cut me to get the baby out. By then, I was exhausted, and I had no strength to push him out. They had me on so much medication I barely knew what was happening to me. It wasn't long, and one black-haired, very hairy and blue-eyed baby boy was born. The only thing I remember was them sitting him on my tummy and looking at his blue eyes and that thick black hair, and then I was out of it for two days.

I was fighting for my life. My whole body was like a balloon. I was under heavy sedation to try to help the preeclampsia to get under control. Apparently, they would bring my baby up to me and latch him onto me, and he would feed. I don't remember a lot of that. It was what I was told happened. Once again, my life could have been taken, but it wasn't. I could barely move my hands with the swelling being so bad. I remember waking up after a couple of days and just feeling soreness everywhere from being cut in labour and pain from the swelling.

I was literally handed my baby and was expected to look after him. I cried a lot. I didn't know how to breastfeed, and it was becoming painful. I went home with this new little baby, but I was not enjoying motherhood. I associated breastfeeding with pain, and every feeding had me tense with fear. My baby was not latching on properly and had just about destroyed my breasts. I couldn't keep going.

I decided to go to the doctors and ask about bottle feeding. So, I decided to stop breastfeeding and bottle-feed him. I was a changed person. I felt relief with my decision and never looked back. My little boy was very placid in his personality, except for the projectile vomiting he did. Finally, I started enjoying being a mother for the first time.

Things were going so well that we decided to try for another baby. I fell pregnant straight away. I ended up with preeclampsia again, so I was induced at thirty-eight weeks. I had to have an epidural again, and my waters were broken.

Seventeen months after having my second little boy, Joel, I had another precious little boy with a totally opposite personality but still beautiful in every way. With this baby, Benjamin, I was able to breastfeed, which was an answer to one of my prayers. After what happened with James, I thought I would not be able to nurse, but it was so different. I don't know if it was that I felt I had more confidence because he was my second child who I was physically looking after, but I never had any issues, and the experience was beautiful. I was so thankful to God for it.

Nineteen months after my third little boy, I really wanted to try for a little girl. I got down on my knees beside my bed, pouring my heart out to God for a little girl. God answered my prayer, and I was pregnant with a little girl ten months after our third boy. The pregnancy was different from those with my boys. I had severe morning sickness all the way through. It was that fact that made me think it was a girl because, during all three pregnancies with the boys, I had morning sickness but only until halfway through. I found it hard having two little boys and being so sick with the pregnancy and needing to look after them.

I was visiting a girlfriend in the hospital I was going to have my little girl in. I didn't know what was about to happen, and yet again, I was nearly going to lose my life. I was standing near my friend's hospital bed looking at her baby, and all of a sudden, I started feeling dizzy. At first, I didn't want to tell anyone. I had a gut instinct that things weren't good. It got so bad, I felt like the whole room started spinning, so I decided to tell one of the nurses what was happening. I also shared with them my previous history of preeclampsia.

The first thing they did was take my blood pressure, and sure enough, I had preeclampsia again. It was severe to the point everything felt like a whirlwind for the next couple of days. I was admitted to the hospital urgently, and within half an hour was being induced. I was staring death in the eyes yet again.

My baby girl was also at risk of losing her life as she was six weeks premature. I was given an epidural and sedated once again. I had my baby girl, but I never got to hold her. She was taken straight off to a NICU. Both our lives were up in the air for a couple of days. Everything seemed to settle quickly from the preeclampsia, and I was told to go home. I was in shock. I thought they were joking because they were keeping my baby in the hospital. I wanted to breastfeed her. I couldn't understand how they could do that. I mean, a mother should be with her baby. I wasn't allowed to touch her for a few days, either. She was in a glass incubator with heaters and lights. They had this mesh thing over her head to keep her eyes closed. I was not able to bond with her at the start like I did with my boys. She was being fed through a tube on powdered formulae to start.

I said I wanted to breastfeed, so they said I would need to use a breast pump to express my milk. So, I did, but barely any milk would come out. I was sent home with a breast pump and no baby. I was told to come in every day after the third day, and I could start breastfeeding her.

I also had two little boys who needed looking after at home. I used to try to get into the hospital by 6 a.m., but I remember once I was five minutes late because I had to go to the toilet. I was dragged over the coals by the nurse on duty at the time for being five minutes late. I felt humiliated. I was in a very stressed state because no milk would come out, and I was also told off for that as well. Nearly dying, having a premature baby, who also nearly died, having two little boys at home, and having to drive back and forth to the hospital a couple of times a day was taking a toll on me. All the stress was stopping my milk coming in.

It finally came to the day I could hold my daughter and bond with her. My breast milk started flowing, and nursing my daughter became enjoyable. She was released from the hospital earlier than I thought she would be—seven days after being born.

Life was pretty busy, as I didn't really have any outside help with my children. I was living on the farm still and pretty much isolated. I had to learn to cope on my own as when Wes was at work, and it was just my children and me. My little girl had decided to stop breastfeeding herself at nine months of age. I wasn't producing enough milk due to just being so busy with three children. The last time I nursed her, I cried. I knew it was the last time I would breastfeed her. It made me feel rejected as a mum because all I wanted to do was be able to feed my baby until she was twelve months old. I wished deep down I had help from grandparents, but that wasn't available because of one issue or another. I also thought she would be my last baby because, at that stage, I had had four children in fewer than five years. I can say after seeing my boys have such a close relationship together, I longed for another little girl so they would have each other growing up.

Well, God must have heard my inner heart. About thirteen months later, after my first little girl, I was pregnant with what would be my last child. The pregnancy was the same as the previous one. I had morning sickness all the way through. This pregnancy was very hard, with three little ones to look after. I lived at the toilet. At one stage, I had three sets of eyes staring at me, asking me, 'Mummy, are you all right?' It nearly made me laugh—if I hadn't been so sick.

Things were desperate. I used to have all my children on routines with sleep times, and I found this helped a lot. I remember at one point I felt so exhausted I thought I would lie down for half an hour. I woke up two hours later. My baby girl had fallen asleep in the playpen. My boys had fallen asleep wherever, and I found a half-eaten banana and half-eaten biscuits with a stool up to the pantry cupboard. I felt proud in one way that I knew my kids wouldn't starve. It was so funny, but it was the reality of my life. I had to cope in whatever way I could.

The story of my life happened. I was thirty-eight weeks pregnant, and I got preeclampsia again. I was induced at thirty-eight weeks. I can tell you now this was the first and last normal delivery I ever had. I asked for an epidural because I knew nothing else, as with all of my other pregnancies, I'd had an epidural. But my last little girl was in a hurry to enter the world. An hour and a half after being induced, she was born. With a couple of quick pushes, she was out. I went into shock. I delivered her, and they gave her straight to me.

All four of my other children were taken from me as soon as they were born due to complications and preeclampsia. I expected the same, but everything was all right with her, and for the first time, I was handed my baby to lay on my chest and hold. It was precious, especially as she was the last child I was going to have. I was so thankful to God for my four blessings after losing my first little boy.

••• 8 •••

Lost Without My Children

So here I was with four children under the age of five. My life was crazy busy. I was still home on the farm with no outside help except for Wes in the evenings. I had to put my children on routines to cope, which helped a lot. There was always a lot going on with the farm work that kept Wes busy. I loved sewing and making my children's clothes when they were younger. I think back now and wonder how I had the time to do what I did. I knew I wanted to be able to do for my children all I dreamed of as a little girl and couldn't have or experience. I organised incredible parties, made the most extravagant cakes, and poured my heart into my children. I continued making clothes for them. My children were my life, my all.

I used to have to take all four children shopping by myself. It was quite hard at times, but my children knew if they acted up when we were out, they would get in trouble when we got home. Knowing I wasn't going to have more children, I wasn't in a rush to put my youngest girl onto solid foods. I was still nursing her up until fifteen months of age. She was intolerant to all foods, I discovered.

One Christmas Eve, she was rushed into the Royal Children's Hospital to get a bone-marrow test because they thought she had a rare cancer. She had many tests done, and they could not find out what was wrong. So, over the next few months, I had to take her through a very slow, hard process of introducing one new food, starting with just one teaspoon of it for a few days. If she didn't react, I was allowed to introduce another new food to her. It took months until she could eat like a typical child could.

When my eldest was old enough to start kindergarten, we had to make a decision on how the children would be schooled. The church we were in at the time pushed heavily that home-schooling was a must, and most of the families did home-schooling. I decided to try it. I didn't really know what I was doing to start with, so I would ask advice from other mums at church. My youngest little girl was just a baby, and my oldest was in kindergarten.

I enjoyed doing kindergarten with my oldest child. To start with, I only did a couple of hours with him. One-on-one, I seemed to get a lot done. I enjoyed preparing his work and all it involved. The next year, I had my oldest boy in prep and my second boy in kindergarten. It was more challenging.

My oldest boy seemed to learn quickly, and I just assumed all children were the same until my second boy. There were no books to tell me how to teach children to learn in different ways. I think I placed expectations on my second boy, and it took me a while to learn that all children need to be taught differently.

I had never gone to university to learn how to become a teacher; I just asked a lot of questions from other mums. Home-schooling opened my eyes to how different children are, that some are creative with their hands, and some are creative in their minds. With my second son, I felt I was similar to him, as I am very creative with my hands like he is. But academically, I found it harder to teach a child who was creative. I had to learn more hands-on ways of teaching.

When it came time to teach my first little girl, my third child, I was feeling stretched. Fortunately, the oldest little girl was like the oldest boy. She took straight to everything. Having her like that, soaking in everything, helped me a lot because I needed more time with my second boy in preparing lessons differently. Then two years later, I started teaching my youngest little girl in prep.

Having four children being home-schooled was one of the most challenging experiences academically I had faced. I was generally a very quiet person, but the stress of teaching four children became a yelling match. I struggled to get my mind to change to where each of the children was at in their book work, and I struggled with the pace of it all. My youngest daughter was like my second son, and it was harder for me to find ways to teach her. I would have to stay with my youngest, and if I had time, help my second son. The other two children I felt like I was neglecting because there were four of them and only one of me.

All my school holidays were spent preparing lessons for the term ahead, so I never felt like I was enjoying it anymore. I felt angry because I couldn't cope with the pressure of teaching four children incurred. I felt like I had to decide to put the children into school. I felt like they were struggling because I wasn't coping. It was a hard decision to make.

All I knew was bringing up my four children. Every day they were my life. I felt like my heart was being torn in two. I felt like I was failing as a mum, but I couldn't keep going like I was. I feared what others would think about me for stopping the home-schooling. I know some thought it was better I put them into school, but what was ripping my heart up was parting from my children. My oldest was ten years old by then, so for ten years, all I had known in my life was my children. I started looking at schools and quickly decided I wanted them in a private school. There were no schools close to the farm. I ended up finding a Christian school that I would have to drive them to. They all had to be tested to see what grade they would go into. The oldest boy and girl were way above Australian standards of teaching because I had been using an American curriculum. The youngest girl tested below the standards to go into the grade she should have—she was kept down a level. I blamed myself for that. I just kept thinking if I could have done things differently, she would have gone into the grade she should have been in had she not been home-schooled.

My children were slowly introduced to mainstream schooling by attending three separate days over the last term of the school year. That seemed to help them a lot. In January the following year, it was time for school. Something major happened to me. I came home to a deadly quiet house, and I felt like my children had been taken from me, I felt like a failure at the thought I couldn't keep home-schooling. For the first term, I had my youngest daughter home with me in the middle of the week, and I loved that fact. It broke my loneliness. We would do special activities together. I looked forward to those days.

I noticed a culture shock for my children once they were in school. There were many issues that needed to be tackled. On the farm, I never put my children in lace-up shoes because it was too hard with four little children who had to go out quickly. So, slip-on shoes were all they wore to save me time. My oldest daughter wrote on a tree and received detention for it. On the farm, we carved little messages on trees or love hearts and never thought anything of it. I hadn't taught my children about what graffiti was, so I had to teach them and to tie shoelaces up for the first time. There were many other issues, also. With home-schooling, my children could get up early and finish their schoolwork by lunchtime, and we didn't necessarily take breaks. The schooling would be done, and then they could play. At school, there was morning tea, lunchtime, and afternoon tea. My children realised after not a long period that mainstream schooling was way longer in hours and had no time left in their days to play. They came home after their long days and still had homework. They went from having a five- to six-hour day to about a twelve-hour day. My children were struggling with this, and so was I. I felt torn. I wasn't coping with teaching them, but I also knew I had to put them in school. After the first term of school had finished, my youngest daughter was then in school full-time. The reality had hit me. I felt so lonely. I would cry all day; for weeks that happened. The guilt I was carrying was heavy. I felt lost and without a purpose. I felt I had let down my children not being a good enough mum to keep home-schooling.

The ripping going on in my heart was so painful. It wasn't long before I had realised my marriage was a mess as well. The children were my life, my marriage had been neglected and covered up by having my children there, and now I was at the loneliest time in my life—no children and a marriage that was broken. *And who was I? What was I going to do with my life now?* This year ten girl who was told to leave school because she was too dumb was broken, lost, and hurting. I started on a search for who I was and what I wanted to do with my life. This search led to dark places all in the name of trying to find love.

••• 9 •••

I'm Leaving You, God

The church our family belonged to at the time had split, and one group of parishioners had formed another church. There was a lot of insecurity of thoughts whirling around in my mind. My husband and I decided to go to the new church.

Originally the church seemed all right, but as time went on, I felt it became cultish in some ways, and I was expected to choose certain people's ways of doing things and what they said I should do. I didn't really think about choosing for myself. I followed what most others were choosing to do out of fear. The fear was that I would be looked down on, and it made me feel isolated and alone. I didn't want to be the odd one out, so I chose to do what everyone else was doing without questioning, even though deep in my heart, I was probably resenting what I was doing.

One of the issues that played on my mind was that it seemed as though having a simple Christmas tree was the biggest sin in the world, and I missed having one. I had fond memories of when we use to decorate the tree together as a family with my siblings. I didn't recall a lot of great memories growing up, but I loved Christmas, and I loved going to a Christmas tree farm with my family each year to pick out a special one. For me, it felt like the church was ripping away one of the few good memories I had from my childhood.

Another issue was that most of the parents in that particular church home-schooled their children, and if you were to ask me at that time what I thought about doing it, I was petrified. Once again, I played the game of following the leader and did what everyone else was doing instead of thinking for myself or even asking God what He truly wanted me to do.

There were many other issues with the church, but many people—including me—chose simply to do what everyone else was doing, whether we wanted to or not. Fear had a great effect on me through this period of my life, and I hadn't really thought about questioning anything or anyone. Before I had put any proper thought into all these issues, there was something playing around in my mind about when I was baptised as a nine-year-old girl. I never really understood baptism.

As part of me trying to find who I really was, I decided I wanted to be rebaptised. I wanted to be baptised for the right reasons and understand what it meant. I approached my pastor at the time and asked about being rebaptised, but I felt a coldness towards me from him. I didn't think too much about it until it came to the day of my baptism. I gave my testimony, and I was excited about my decision. When I was baptised, the feeling I got when I spoke to my pastor came again, so I felt discouraged.

After my baptism, I went out to have supper with people who had attended, and many people said to me, 'What was with the coldness in how you were being treated?' In one way, I was glad I wasn't imagining what I was experiencing, but it left me feeling discouraged and wondering why I was being treated as I was. Issues in that church seemed to arise more and more. I felt like I was being particularly isolated and picked on for several different issues.

One issue was that I was falsely accused before the whole church. That broke me more than my words could express. I started feeling angry towards God. I was looking at how people were treating me and not at God. My marriage was struggling, I felt I'd lost my children by putting them into school. My whole life was falling apart.

Being falsely accused by this church was the last straw. I looked at myself as a worthless human being. I looked in the mirror and saw what I thought was ugly. After having my five children, I had been putting on weight after each child and had no self-esteem. I didn't feel I was good enough for my husband. I felt unattractive, unwanted, and unloved.

I started putting my focus into trying to lose weight for all the wrong reasons, and I started to walk each day and change my eating habits. After quite a few months, I had lost twenty kilos. But after I lost that amount, nothing happened for quite some time with additional weight loss. Losing weight seemed to be giving me some confidence back, and I had been putting all my focus in my life at that time into losing weight. I remember seeing a competition in a café to win a gym membership, but I didn't think my husband would let me join it. Here was the beginning of me starting to allow lies to fill my life. I had told my husband I had won this competition for a gym membership. I had become obsessed with going to the gym. I started feeling that I was finding my value in losing weight. I had people commenting about how I looked, and it was filling that hole I had in my heart for a little while. I was going to the gym five days a week, and I was walking twice a day to try to get to the weight I wanted.

I had become so angry with God for what had happened at the church. I felt unfulfilled. My husband and I left the church we were in. It was the first time in my life I wasn't attending a church. I blamed God for not helping me or being there for me in the church when I was falsely accused. But when I look back now, I think I see a build-up of issues happening to me to bring me to the point I was at.

I had an alcoholic father and a mother who didn't know how to love me and had abused me with her forms of discipline. I had a husband who had fallen out of love with me, I had been raped, I had been used by boys and men, I had a disease that crippled my life for a few years, I had lost a child, and now I was falsely accused in my church! I had a hole in my heart that felt as big as a mountain.

I wanted to feel loved, but nothing seemed to fill me. There was only brokenness. Where was love? It seemed to run from me my whole life. Where were you, God? I was so desperate to find love. I figured in my head at the time that if God had deserted me, I was going to desert God once and for all! I screamed and cried, 'Where were you, God when I was getting falsely accused in front of this church?'

Anger towards God filled me, rage even. 'Why would a God who created the universe abandon me?' My whole life, I kept telling myself He was there with me, but now I had nothing left in me to believe that was true. Faith had gone. When I tried to tell the truth in the church, it was like all ears had become deaf. Doors had closed. People's hearts shut off towards me. I felt there was no hope, so I started believing the false accusations of what people said I was. I labelled myself with lies from other people. I couldn't prove to them that they were lying, so I thought I'd give up and be that person.

So, with so much anger towards God, I told God I was leaving Him. I told God that if He wasn't going to help me or love me, I was going to worship Satan, and so I did. The hurt inside me was tremendous for me to take such a step. I had no idea what I was stepping into just by saying I was going to worship Satan. That was the start of one of the hardest journeys I was going to experience in my life—all because I chose to believe in lies about myself instead of God's truths.

••• 10 •••

Eight Years in the Wilderness

It started with lies other people said about me. I was being labelled wayward, adulterous woman. Never in a million years would I have thought I would walk down the track I was about to. I always thought that was for other people. Both my parents had walked down this track, and I thought I would never follow in their footsteps. I'd been to church pretty much my whole life.

Here is how it started, as in the physical steps I started taking to walking the life I was accused of living. I used to walk every day for my exercise, and at the time, there was a freeway being built, so there were lots of men working. There was one man in particular who started chatting to me and complimenting how I looked with the way I was losing weight. I started to enjoy the attention. I started to look forward to my walks each day, hoping I would meet up with the man paying me compliments. Time went on, and our conversations got deeper. We could both feel an attraction forming. I just wanted to feel loved.

But something else happened. I was stuck in a park with this man with no one else around. I was asked to do something that was humiliating, but I was scared he would do something to me. I felt sick and humiliated, used, and rejected. This man who I thought was my friend had come with only one intention—to use me. I was in shock and crying and was told afterwards by him that things would go no further. I couldn't tell anyone because I was the one who had organised with him to meet.

I went home with a pain the size of the universe in my heart. Rejection became the driving force in my life to find some sort of love that could fulfil. This man told me about what I could do to fulfil myself to find someone else, and that was to ring a chat line to talk with other guys. I'd never done it before, and it was something I was craving—just to be listened to, to be loved. The men were degrading, all wanting only one thing. I wanted something else. I wanted to be loved, and it looked like I was going to have to give of myself in order just to get conversation and feel loved. I honestly did not want to walk this road, but the pain in my heart to find fulfilling love pushed me. It pushed me into darkness, and I was going to find love no matter the cost.

I decided to look for a job. I wanted some independence to be able to do the things I wanted. It was a big issue for me because I hadn't really worked in a proper job since I was eighteen years old, and I doubted that I would get employment. I used to go into this lingerie shop often, and the lady told me I should apply for the job. I thought she was joking. In my mind, I thought, *Why would you employ me?* I went for the interview, and surprisingly enough, I got the job. I had a love for lingerie at the time, and this seemed to impress the company.

Not being in the workforce for so many years, I realised a lot had changed. People's attitudes had changed. Ethics had changed. Computers had been introduced to retail, and it wasn't just a cash register like back when I worked years ago. It was a totally new thing with me. I had no idea how to use one. Over time I eventually learnt, and it built my confidence in myself.

Not being around other women much except for women at church on Sundays, I found it hard seeing how different women from a church treated me and women who had not been in a church treated me. It was a bit of a culture shock. I had been living on the farm since I was eighteen with no people around except my husband and children. Because of the pain in my heart in trying to find love, I embraced anything new, chasing it in whatever forms it came, hoping it would fill my pain.

During the time I was working, I continued to go to the gym. I got compliments from people, but it never lasted. I wanted more and more attention. My body looked the best it ever had in my life! I had been lifting weights, my body had toned, and I had lost forty kilos! I had also been offered a job to do modelling at age thirty-six. It brought memories back from when I was sixteen, and I was offered a modelling job. It felt like a second chance, and I thought maybe it would help fill that hole in my heart.

The attention I was receiving from men was pulling on my heartstrings. It was making me feel special and appreciated. I loved doing the modelling even though I didn't take it that far as in paid work. I had a professional album made. My whole life, I had been teased for being overweight and ugly, and here I was at age thirty-six having a modelling job. It felt like for once in my life, all the pain of being teased had somehow been relieved. It was like I could announce to the world,

'Look at me now, all of you who teased me. Look at my body now.' I felt like I had some sort of control back over my life.

I had created an addiction, though. I transferred my pain into something other than God. Like everything else in the world, vanity and attention only fill your heart for a quick fix. Nothing in the world has eternal value unless it's from God and his heart. I had to learn the hard way and do things my way, not God's way.

I had my job, I had my gym, and I had my modelling, but it wasn't filling me. I remember going up to my husband and telling him I was getting attention from other men, but I don't feel he believed me. To me, in my warped way of thinking, I took that as a green light. It was as if I'd done my job telling him what is happening, and if he didn't care, well, that wasn't my problem. I took it as rejection that he didn't care about what was happening to me, and it just added to the big mountain of rejection I had received my whole life.

What my inner heart was doing was crying, *Come rescue me*. Even though by this point, I had left God, it felt like a last desperate plea for help that never came. So, I had to continue to try to find my own way of discovering real love somewhere, somehow, someplace. The places I was led to in my near future were at this time places I wouldn't send a dog, let alone a human, but this is what happens when God is gone in your life. Darkness takes over. You can't see past lies. You believe any lies from the past that people have said about you. I took the hand of darkness itself, and darkness became the lover of my soul.

••• 11 •••

Love, Lust, and Betrayal

On the chat line, I had discovered many men, but one caught me in his web. He was on the prowl and was looking for a naive girl, and he certainly found her. He spoke to me so persuasively. He said all the right things at the right times. After about two and a half weeks of chatting with this man, and I thought I was in love. I told him after three weeks that I was in love with him. I think that scared him off. He went quiet on me for a few weeks.

I was so desperate to find love; all it took was someone giving me constant attention for a few days, and I was gone. I had bought a phone which I had hid from my husband to use to chat with other men. This phone became such a source of evilness to me in many ways. I had so quickly entrusted my heart to another man without any clear thinking. I had been deceived by him saying he wasn't in any serious relationship, and for me, that was an open door. I can't express in words how blind I was to how I was running my heart on my feelings and not God's truths. My head was saying to chase this love, and that was exactly what I needed to fill me. I couldn't hear my heart because I had chosen to block out God's voice with the world.

After a few weeks, this guy started talking to me again, but with me feeling broken because he just disappeared, I started to chase other men. The pain of rejection cut deeper and deeper with each blow, driving me towards Satan and begging him to give me things to make me feel happy. But Satan wouldn't just give things out without you giving back to him. Satan would fill your mind with false promises, making you believe if you did what he said, you would get what you asked. He would literally deceive me. I would do whatever he asked because he would dangle the so-called beautiful fruit in front of my eyes, and I would be totally fixed on the outward beauty of inward rot.

I found another man who said he used to go to church, and that drew me in a bit because I thought he might understand me. So, one night I had bought a great big bottle of vodka to drink. The only thing I happened to know about vodka was that people could not smell it on your breath. I had no idea how much one person should drink. I, being naïve, drank half a big bottle of vodka. In my drunken state, I gave myself to this man.

I was taken home and could barely walk. I sat on the side of my bed and could not move! I vomited everywhere but could not move. I never realised until years later that I should have died that night. The blood poisoning, I had from alcohol was way over my limit. The next day my husband came home, and I lied to him and said I had gastro upset.

My life was one big constant string of lies that seemed to have no end. Once I started with one lie, I would tell other lies to cover the initial ones. That was the first time I had been fully and physically unfaithful in my marriage. My mind was already unfaithful, but now my acts of living were, too. What the church had accused me of was now living truth, and there was no turning back. I became who they said I was—an adulterer.

This one drunken night of lust came with a price that I didn't know at the time. I contracted a sexually transmitted disease, a sentence that will stay with me until I die. I was infected with HPV, and it never goes away. It stays in your blood, and whenever it wants to rear its ugly head, it does. There is no cure for it; it is a sentence that will always remind you of your mistake. The only way to treat it is by creams or pills that usually don't work or another much harsher treatment: going to the doctor, who uses liquid nitrogen to burn it off! I would walk into the doctor's office, already humiliated because of the act of committing what I did. You leave any dignity of any sort at the doctor's doorway. I can say I thank God for my doctor, Kwai Lee, for her gentle heart and all the patience she's had with me and through everything she's seen me go through. She truly still shows me love and care without judgment all the way through.

After a few weeks of treatment, it went away. It came back again, and I went through the whole process again. Then in August 2018, it came back and has not gone yet. I had not had the disease for three years, and suddenly it turned up again. When it first came back, I was devastated. All my memories of my past came flooding back. I felt dirty and humiliated, and I had a million questions for God. I felt I would never get rid of that name—adulterer! But I will share later in my story about this area of my life.

So, here I was with two guys on the scene at once in my life. One in another state and one close by me. I had a lot of pain in me from the man from interstate because I had fallen in love with him (lust, as I realize now). This man who had my heart started telling me about other relationships he had been in, so I thought I would tell him as payback for hurting me how I had slept with the other guy. I thought, *If you are going to hurt me by telling me how you were with others, I will hurt you back and tell you what I have been doing.*

Well, of course, he disappeared again for a few weeks. Then the local guy also cooled down off me. I was feeling more and more rejected each day. I thought, *Well, if those guys are gone, I will find someone else.* So I did. By now, there was no thought of God in me. I had walked the path I thought no one could ever come back from. I found more men and had more conversations, wanting to find love.

I had lost sight of even thinking there was anything of value left. I contemplated becoming a prostitute. I was offered money a couple of times but never went through with it. Many times, I thought about walking naked out on the freeway near where I lived and in front of a car to kill myself.

By now, it had been about six weeks, and the interstate man had decided to contact me yet again. He was all apologetic for not messaging me back and ignoring me. I fell back into his trap yet again. You may notice a pattern evolving here in my story of what I kept doing. I kept going back to what was destroying me. I was trapped.

This time I felt the guy from interstate was genuine. He pulled all my heartstrings. I had decided I was leaving my husband to be with this man. I had even packed my bags and had them ready, hidden in the wardrobe. My heart was so sick with selfishness I wasn't even thinking about my children, only what my heart was lusting after.

Then I received a phone call from the interstate guy. He said his girlfriend, who wasn't supposed to be anything serious, was pregnant. I was devastated. I had planned my life out, and all had changed within one phone call. I know when I look back that this was God's hand.

This man had me under such a trance that when he told me nothing would change between him and me, I believed him. He had me eating out of the palm of his hand, so to speak. When I look back now, this man had a narcissistic personality that explained the control he had over me, but I let him control me.

I got to the point that I praying to Satan for him to let me live with this man, and I was willing to do anything he asked. It was at this point that Satan wanted me to pledge my soul to him. That was the worst step I ever took in my life. It was like I did not have a mind of my own. I could never think logically. I became a person who had no fear of anything I did. Suicide and depression thoughts were always in my mind. I couldn't see at the time that Satan would never give me what I wanted. He just knew how to deceive me to get me to do things.

I would check the star signs and search for tarot card readers. I always wanted to know my future. I bought any trashy magazines that had anything to do with readings or tarot readings. I was always concerned about how I looked and what I wore. One thing I felt Satan wanted from me was that I keep myself looking really good because it attracted people to me.

Yet, despite everything I was doing, I could see the trace of God's hand. Before I had walked away from God, I had memorised eight chapters of Proverbs. The verses from Proverbs about being an adulterer would whisper to me. It would make me angry that I could still hear them. I would tell God I was not his anymore.

I had this constant goal of trying to seek a life of being with this man who was interstate. It had been two years since we had started talking, and I was determined to finally find a way to meet this man. I used to go to the gym and then straight to work. I made up a lie to my husband and said I had won this competition through my company for a trip to Sydney. Then I told uncountable lies to bring this about.

At this time in my life, lies were a way of living. I had barely any conscience left of anything that I was doing was wrong in any way. I finally got to meet this man, and I thought I was more in love with him than I had ever been. All I could think of was how I could be with him. By this time, he had the woman who had gotten pregnant living with him, and they had a daughter. He kept telling me they weren't in love, and he was doing what he was because he felt trapped and had no choice. I believed him.

I could see he was not happy in his relationship, and that's how I would justify myself. I was not happy, and he was not happy. He started getting into all sorts of experimental sexual things that became out of control. He was addicted to pornography and pursuing anything physically involved with it. That is what led me to what I call 'the black hole'.

••• 12 •••

The Black Hole

This became what would be the darkest, most evil time in my life. I was constantly depressed, and I had let this man take control of me. I wanted to be with him so badly, and he had started losing interest in me, so I was looking for any way that would make him want me or want to keep me.

He would punish me at times by not returning messages or phone calls for days or even weeks on end. I started trying to impress him by buying lavish things for him, hoping this would make him love me, but he was getting further and further from liking me.

One thing that drew him to me was his addiction to sexual activities, so I started involving myself in anything that gave him pleasure. I became a slave to feed his ego, but I didn't care. I started drinking a lot around this time as the depression grew deeper. I would drink vodka, so the smell wouldn't be detected on me. I kept buying more and more lingerie to try and impress this guy in Sydney. He started involving himself in many different relationships at the same time. I pretended to be happy, but I was dying inside.

I started being involved in many relationships at one time also. I wanted to keep up with him and make him think he needed me. Out of pain and desperation, I let men use me and abuse me, still hoping that maybe I would find just one man who could love me. My pain grew deeper.

I really started having hate towards men and thought, *Well, if men can't fulfil me, I will try women.* So, I started walking down the road of pursuing relationships with women. In my head, I thought they wouldn't hurt me like men did. I started associating myself more with gay people, and I would spend time with them, talk to them, and ask them how they made their decisions to become gay. What I heard was that many had chosen a connection with the same sex because of pain from previous relationships gone wrong with opposite-sex people.

The women I found ended up treating me worse than men did if that was possible! Rejection with a capital 'R' was my life. There seemed to be no love anywhere, with anyone. My drinking had gotten heavier, and without my knowing, I had started doing damage to my gallbladder. I had started becoming severely depressed and suicidal. I was letting myself be used as a puppet by the guy in Sydney, and I was living at my doctor's office. I started sharing with her how depressed I was. She became very concerned for my wellbeing and kept trying to persuade me to see a psychologist. At my wit's end, I eventually relented and started seeing a psychologist, not knowing things were about to get even worse for me.

The guy in Sydney did more things that seemed to crush me continually. He became my constant point of wanting to end my life. Attempts to take my life started taking place. I would get sharp knives out at home to do something, but somehow something would always stop me. Between my doctor and my psychologist, I ended up on antidepressants. They would make me tired and want to sleep all the time, but it was either that or not be living. My psychologist and doctor were trying to get me to see the reality of my life and that the dreams I was hoping for were simply not realistic, but I did not want to listen, no matter what they said.

I was under Satan's control, and I had sold my soul to him. He had control over my life. Many times, men would use me and just leave me lying on a motel bed, all used like a rag doll. I would lay there crying in such deep pain and only wanting to be loved. I felt like I was begging for someone to see my inner heart and not my external appearance. But it didn't happen. Not yet.

I became really sick one night, and I had to ring for an ambulance. I was in so much pain in my stomach, it felt like a horse had come and was inside my gut kicking me. As pain hit, I would smash my head against the floor to try to combat the pain. My kids saw me lying on the floor like this. I can't imagine what went through their minds. I was taken to Dandenong Hospital, and they first thought I had gallstones. I saw my doctor, Luke Crantock. This man had journeyed with me for many years and was encouragement in my life whenever I saw him all through my health issues. I became worse, and they discovered I had pancreatitis.

Something happened that I will not ever forget one night I got so sick. I felt my body shutting down. I laid my head to the side and was choking from my vomit, not having the strength to even lift my head. All of a sudden, there was staff around me. For a brief moment, my spirit came out of my body, and I was watching myself. I looked like I was dying. I wanted to die. I had had enough. But I remember hearing a voice saying, 'It's not your time yet'. Everything in me wanted to die, but God had other plans.

It was when I was in the hospital that I was caught being unfaithful by my husband for the first time. I wanted him to tell me to leave. It would be my ticket to freedom, but he chose still to want me. I was not ready to acknowledge any of my sins. I still wanted to live a life of lies. My husband tried for a few weeks, but he was trying in his own strength, and things between us weren't genuine. Neither of us had found our way back to God, and within weeks of trying to fix things on my husband's part, we were right back where we started.

I recovered from nearly dying and still kept pursuing this guy in Sydney. I thought I would do the most amazing thing for this man. When it came to his birthday, I was going to give him a birthday no man would ever forget. I decked out a hotel room with everything: balloons, cake, his favourite alcohol. I made a blanket by hand and had it posted up to Sydney. I had all the food you could think of put in the room. I did whatever I could to think I could buy his love. I poured my heart into him. I returned home, and he decided afterwards that he wouldn't speak to me for weeks. I became suicidal. I drove my car once at one hundred-and-forty miles per hour and was intending to end my life, but all I can say was it was like an angel grabbed my car and pulled me to a halt. I had my foot on the accelerator and was coming up to a roundabout. I was going to hit whatever car entered, but God intervened once again.

Another time, I was at my mother-in-law's place. While everyone was out, I went to the kitchen to grab a knife and end my life. But somehow, I ended up in bed and on the phone to my psychologist. I told her I wanted to end my life, and the next minute the local police were ringing my mother-in-law's place to check on me. I lied again to my family and pretended nothing was wrong, but inside, my heart was crumbling, and I didn't want to live.

Once I even travelled halfway around the world to see this man. I turned up in Sydney, and he said he could only see me for an hour as some issues happened at work. My heart was worse than shattered. I was hurting so badly from how I was being treated by this guy that I wanted to start hurting him back for all the pain he had caused in my life.

So, one of the times I saw him, I thought up the perfect lie (Well, I thought it was back then). I told him I was pregnant with his child. This act got his attention quickly, and he would message me every day. But he said he never wanted the baby. I thought back then I had something that would finally make him want to keep me. I said to him I would have the baby aborted because I wanted to make him happy. He was happy with my decision, and I kept stringing him on for weeks with this story, lapping up all the attention I was receiving. I thought if someone was willing to sacrifice the life of a child, he would surely love me then. I pretended to go through with what he thought was having an abortion.

He was messaging me, saying he was throwing up and hated that I had to do this. I was loving the fact that he was finally feeling some pain after all he had done to me. The very next day after the supposed abortion, he then again stopped talking to me. What I thought would win his heart just made him push me away even more.

After a few weeks, he decided to contact me again. He wanted to see me, so I went up to Sydney again. On my walk back onto the aeroplane, I turned my head and looked back. In my gut, I felt it would be the last time I would see him. And it was.

I found out he had another girlfriend on top of me and the one he was living with at his house. Then it turned out the newest girlfriend got pregnant and had a baby boy by him. I spoke to him on and off for several more years, and all I heard from him was how many people in his life he was continually hurting. I pretended I agreed with all he was doing. I would get phone numbers of people and started talking to them and found out even deeper lies of how many people he had been hurting.

I ended up talking to his two other girlfriends, and the stories I heard were just heartbreaking. I became friends with these two women and became a shoulder they could cry on. I knew their pain. I'd walked in it. The two girlfriends who had his children became bitter with each other and jealous. After some time, everyone stopped talking. There was too much pain for anyone to handle. We all went our own ways. The last I heard was that the woman he was living with was destroying things in their house to pay him back for the pain he caused her. The other woman with the baby boy was trying to get money from him to bring up their child. It became a big mess.

I had started having some back issues, and it got to the point that I had to stop working. I could no longer even walk, and nobody knew what was wrong with me. I had to get help going to the toilet, and if I could walk there would be involuntary screams from the excruciating pain. God had me in a place where I had to just stop everything I was doing, which took up about eighteen months of my life. For six months of it, I spent in bed pretty much not being able to walk. I had a lot of time to think, but my heart was still hardened. I thought, *My heart is as hard as Pharaoh's was in the Bible.* I was so stubborn and did not want to come back to God.

They finally found out what was wrong with my back after I saw seven specialists. I had some tell me it was in my head again the pain I was having. It felt like revisiting my past. They said my muscles in my spine had collapsed, and when I stood up, there was nothing to support me when I was walking. A decision was made that I would start physical therapy. I had already spent thousands of dollars at a specialist chiropractor, but nothing changed. Within a month of going to physical therapy, I was walking again. You would think after all I'd been through; I would surely have turned back to God, but my heart still was not ready.

••• 13 •••

My Marriage Was Over

When I finally started walking again, it didn't take me long before that part of my heart that was not fulfilled was still looking to be filled. God desperately tried to soften my heart during the time I couldn't walk, but it fell on deaf ears and blind eyes still. My hardened heart had not budged; it had just been laid to rest for a few months.

My brother had his wedding in Sydney, and I was asked to go. I really wanted my husband to come with me because it was going to be an emotional time. For the first time in thirteen years, my parents were going to be together at this wedding. They had decided to put their differences aside to come together for an event. After the second divorce of my parents, there was a lot of bitterness and unresolved pain. Some of my siblings had been through their own divorces and pain. It seemed to be everywhere in my family.

I had wanted my husband to come with me for support, but because it was Sydney, and I had a history there, he could not bring himself to come. Which I understood. The wedding day came, and I was shaking and nervous from the thought of seeing my parents together after so many years. I saw their eyes meet. I saw the pain in their hearts still, and I can honestly tell you that the same thought of me wanting my parents back together from when I was a little girl still flickered in my heart.

I have always hated broken things, whether it be material things or relationships. I think that part in me comes from Jesus; He wants to repair the broken people of this world. I hate seeing broken people.

I watched them eye each other. I was going back and forth as a mediator between them, trying to get them to talk to each other. My mum was nervous, and so was my dad. Eventually, they approached each other, and after thirteen years, the ice was broken. They started talking. I remember going inside the house where the reception was being held and shoving myself in a corner and crying my heart out. It was a mixture of pain and happiness.

I got the courage to ask if my parents would have a photo taken with me, and they let me. It meant the world to me. Seeing my parents talk after all those years was wonderful, but the pain of seeing their brokenness hurt me. I wanted so desperately to talk to someone about my pain, so I tried to ring my husband and reach out to him, but he was barely coping with the fact I was in Sydney. He wasn't in a place to reach out and comfort me while his own heart was struggling.

I felt alone and isolated. The pain inside me was rising. At this time in my life, God was still not there. I had not returned to Him. As a creature of habit, I did what my brain did in the past. I went on a chat line and started talking with another man. It didn't take long, and I connected very quickly. Again, I was deceived because he said all the right things that pulled on my heart chords. Had I been with Jesus, I would have known I could have called on Him at any time.

Because I had placed expectations on my husband about being there for me when my heart was falling apart, I chased something else to try to fill my pain yet again. When my husband didn't meet this need, it was truly the last straw for me in our marriage. I was exhausted from trying to repair a marriage so broken. To me, there was nothing left.

It had been about three weeks, and I had fallen in love—or I thought I had—again. I started really pursuing this man. I decided to meet up with him, and I could see it didn't seem right, but my void needed filling. The black hole in me needed feeding continually. If I didn't feed it, I would feel pain. This man ironically had the same personality as the Sydney man: narcissistic and very controlling. I seemed to fall for these types of men because they had a way with words that drew me in.

I started living as I was before I hurt my back—a life of lies and covering things up. I started getting involved in this other man's life and family and getting attached. It wasn't long before I noticed this man's personality was so similar to the man in Sydney. He was involved with other women and would deny it. It was the same story all over again! I became chained.

It's like I could see issues but was blinded and didn't want to face the reality of the truth. I was creating my own pain through denial. This man was treating me badly, and I let him. I started getting depressed again and suicidal. When I was in these places of depression and suicidal thoughts, it's like something took over my mind, and it didn't want to let in any light or truth.

I was tired all the time. I was very self-focused. Life was always about what I wanted and how I felt. My life revolved around myself. It's like everyone else in the world didn't matter. I got to a place of such selfishness that I didn't think about my children, and I never thought about my husband and all the pain I was causing him. I went for a few months with plans in mind of leaving my husband. I had enough of trying to save our marriage. It felt draining, but that was because I was full of self and not full of Jesus. The love in our marriage seemed to be dead. The relationship had become habitual, not one of sacrifice.

One night I had some swelling start in my face under my chin. It had gotten so big you could barely see the left side of my neck. I was in pain, and my husband took me to the hospital. He went home while I stayed there overnight. I had asked my husband to bring some things out of my handbag to the hospital, but I had left traces of the hidden relationship I was having. My husband found those things, and I received a phone call from him. He said, 'It's over'. I knew straight away what had happened.

There was a deep part of me that was relieved. I had been running and hiding things from my husband for eight years. I wanted it to be over. He was more than angry. No words could really explain his pain. He had a wife that continually hurt him. Out of his pain, he left me at the hospital and said I had to find my own way home. I felt lifeless like someone had taken all the air out of me. I was numb. I rang my mum, and she picked me up from the hospital. They had said I had a blocked salivary gland, which was causing the swelling, and there wasn't much they could do.

I think about the timing of this happening and being caught. As much pain as there is in being caught in a sin, I see it as an act of God trying with all his heart to get me to stop running from him. I came home to the farm and felt sick, but that relief was still there. I had no energy left for arguing or fighting. I just wanted to leave. I slowly got out of my car and walked towards the front door, and my husband stood in the doorway, looking at me. I could barely look at him. I wanted to go into the house and get my stuff and never come back. He stood there with the whites of his eyes gone red and tears flowing. He wanted me back!

••• 14 •••

Hosea Turned Up

As I looked at the tears in my husband's eyes. I was in shock. I felt angry, confused even. *He wanted me back? Why?* I was ready to grab the hand of freedom, and I wanted it. I was tired and did not want to fight for a marriage that was over. As my husband stood in the doorway, I wanted him to move right out of the way and let me walk in and grab my stuff and let me leave. My kids were distraught with tears. As I think back now, the pain they felt must have been horrendous.

I remembered as a little girl how I felt when my parents broke up. Here I was, putting my own children through the same thing, but my heart was so blinded to other people's needs for so long. I never saw their little hearts breaking, but their whole world had fallen apart.

My second son was down the front of our farm property, the day I came back from the hospital. I remember his brokenness as he paced up and down. He had rung a youth group leader to come and pick him up. I remember feeling glad he had someone because I couldn't help him. I was too broken to think straight and too selfish. I can never go back there and fix this pain in my children or my husband. It's etched deep in my memory as a reminder to never go back there again.

I looked at my husband and said, 'Why would you want me back?' He cried and sobbed and begged, saying, 'I felt God didn't want me to give up on our marriage, and I didn't want our children growing up without a mother', but I was angry and wanted him just to let me go. We had tried before to repair our marriage, and it never worked. I had not seen a change in him that had made me believe our marriage was worth saving. I said I wanted to leave, and he was just begging me to stay. I grabbed my belongings and said I needed to go away at least for the night to think. I wanted to go and be with the man I had been having a relationship with. I thought I was going home to end my marriage.

I honestly could not believe he wanted me back. In my mind, at the time, all I could think about was everything I had been doing. *Why would anybody want somebody like me after all I had done?* My husband didn't know all I had done at that time. It felt too horrible to believe it was possible I was worth loving in any way or form. I felt angry tht he wanted to love me. I had told my lover I was leaving my husband to be with him. At first, he seemed happy I had made the decision to stop living a double life. He wanted me to stop hiding my relationship with him.

I came home the next day, and I was very sad to admit I was leaving. Something had happened to my husband over-night, something I had never seen before in him ever. His heart had softened, but the fear of losing me had gripped him ever so tightly. Before I had walked away from God eight years ago, I had been praying my heart out for years that my husband would truly give his heart back to Jesus. I gave up, though, the day I said to my husband I had other men chasing me. I felt like God had never heard those prayers. They disappeared into the air as far as I was concerned.

The day I returned home, I did not know what had happened but saw a change in him that words were hard to express. I saw it but didn't want to believe it. Surely, after all these years, my prayers hadn't been heard. He was desperate to repair our marriage, but I still didn't want to. But something inside me couldn't just break the marriage right off. It was partly seeing my children hurting, and partly that little thought nagging me that my husband wanted me back.

But I had told my lover I was leaving my husband. I was struggling to believe my husband was genuine. He was begging me to go to counselling, and my oldest daughter was too. I really didn't want to, but I had heard if you were going to divorce, you had to go through some counselling before you could get the divorce, so I thought I would just get my husband and my children off my back and just do the counselling sessions.

I went in with the worst attitude. I went thinking I wasn't going to do any talking that it would be just my husband talking. I was an iron-clad lockbox, and nobody was going to open me. I wasn't going to let anybody in, no matter who they were. My counsellor's name was Wyley Hargraves. He was a very gentle and humble person. I wasn't letting him in either. Nobody was getting to my heart. At first, I would bluff my way through the counselling sessions, barely saying anything. I would come out of a session, and my lover would ask me how things went. It was tearing my heart up a bit. I could start to see cracks opening into my iron clad heart.

I didn't want to tell either my husband or my lover what was going on because I couldn't cope with it. I know this may even sound crazy, but I didn't want to hurt either of them. I kept stringing them both along for a while, but my lover grew cold towards me and distancing himself towards me. I wondered if it was ever his intention to want to be with me. There are some things because of being so deep and personal won't be shared because they will be kept between God and myself, but I was treated pretty badly by my lover, God knows, and that's where it will stay. The way I was treated caused a lot of depression. I went to take my life a few times again with this man. I was addicted to something in him that had me chained, and I didn't know how to break the chains. I kept going back and getting hurt over and over.

My husband had been showing signs of consistent change, which shocked me. I still wouldn't budge, though. My heart was still hard, but the cracks were getting bigger. I wanted to move out into our mobile home on the farm. So, every spare minute we had, my husband and I were spending time together fixing this place up. My husband was in so much fear of me moving out that he looked at it like that was going to be the end.

But God was doing something he couldn't see. The mobile home was full of twenty-five years of rubbish, and neither of us had the mental energy to deal with it. So, we had a massive bonfire, and we burnt five big trailer loads of memories. It felt cleansing in a way, and it was an easy way of dealing with it all. As we worked together, memories of when we were first married and how we use to love doing things together in our mobile home came flooding back. They were good memories I had forgotten about. We had enjoyed doing things together in the garden, and here we were doing that again, and it did something to my heart. I know it was God shedding and pushing some more light into the cracks that were opening. I never told my husband, though.

It came to a point in our counselling sessions that I started opening up. One night I dropped the bombshell to my husband of what I had been doing for the last eight years. I told him about all the men and women I had been with, and why I did it, and how broken I was. Then on the way home for the first time in eight years, guilt hit my heart. I was overwhelmed and sick. I never told my husband why, but that night I said I was moving into the mobile home. It was fixed enough I could live in by then.

My husband was devastated at me wanting to move out of the house. He was in tears. I didn't really know what was happening to my heart, and I couldn't put it in words, but I needed to think. We were living separately in the house, but to my husband, at least I was still in the house. He would make me breakfast every morning. He would look after the children. He did whatever he could to pour love on me. I came home one day, and he had fixed all the broken tiles in our bathroom that had been falling apart for years. He put a CD player in the bathroom with a couple of songs on it— 'Everything I Do, I Do It for You', and 'Please Forgive Me'. He had candles lit, and it looked beautiful. He had drawn a bath for me, and it melted my heart. The change in his heart was amazing.

But every night, I would go back over to the mobile home and sleep, and he would walk me over there and hate to leave me. I heard him crying one night outside my bedroom window. The pain he must have endured, God only knows. He couldn't see God working in me, and he was constantly having to live by faith, which was really hurting him. If you looked at the situation outwardly, it looked like he was losing me, but inwardly God was working.

I was in the house one day, and I saw a book on the coffee table. I asked whose it was, and my husband said it was loaned to him from my sister-in-law. I was not normally a book reader, but for some reason, I was drawn to this book. It was called *Redeeming Love* by Francine Rivers. I asked if I could read it and he said yes. For two days, nearly straight without sleep, I could not put this book down. I know now God wanted me to read it, even though it was intended for my husband. It was meant for me.

It was like God had written my story in the book, but it was the Bible story of Hosea and Gomer. I cried, even the characters talked about in the book were nearly identical to people who I had been dealing with in my life. How this book could have gotten into my hands at the time it did was a miracle from God. He knew I'd read it. My husband had not read this book, but yet he was living out the life of Hosea from the Bible: He loved the adulterous woman with an unconditional love that only came from God. Hosea had turned up in my marriage. He was my husband.

••• 15 •••

The Pursuit of God

We will never truly know what God is doing behind the scenes in anyone's life. We can see outwardly what is happening but never the inward battles of the heart and mind. Only God knows. My situation to some extended family and friends looked like it was hopeless, but the battle that was raging in me was intense. I never told a soul what was happening inside me. This I can share. Those that chose to love me unconditionally reached my heart. Those who loved me with conditions pushed me away. God knew I needed to experience His unconditional love, love that could meet me on my broken road. I was in the world. I could not hear God's voice through his word. I could see it in people's actions. If someone was to ask me why I did what I did, I would tell them honestly, I never wanted to be that person. I only wanted to feel love. Physically I wanted to be held, but behind that being held was still wanting to be loved. I looked in all the wrong places. I looked to humans for a love that was supposed to be filled only by God.

God was pursuing me fiercely and gently at the same time. He knew me because, in Psalm 139. it says, 'For you created my inmost being, you knit me together in my mother's womb.' He knew who needed to do things at the right times in the right places. He knew when books were to be left on coffee tables at precisely the right moment. My husband couldn't see the inside of my heart. He didn't know how much God was doing. My conscience had been activated again after many years of living so selfishly. God knew I wasn't broken enough yet, though, to cry out to Him. As the world says, 'I needed to hit rock bottom.'

We continued to go to counselling sessions, and I finally got the courage to go to sessions by myself. My tower was coming down ever so slowly. I had to be in a place I could trust someone. I had not trusted anyone in many years. I remember feeling scared and worried about what my counsellor would say when I shared the things I did, but trust came with a person who was very gentle and loved with God's love unconditionally.

I was still seeing my lover and had my husband trying with everything inside him to win my heart back. In the bigger picture, it wasn't just about two people getting back together. It was about God leaving the ninety-nine to find that one lost sheep who happened to be me. He was climbing every mountain, so to speak to bring me back. My husband knew I was still talking with this man, and it caused great pain in him. I even had my oldest very wise daughter trying to speak into my heart. She would say, 'Mum, why do you need to talk to that man? Why don't you just talk to Dad or to me?' It was driving my conscience crazy and angry. There was nothing like having your young child speak into your heart.

What many people didn't understand was that I had addictions. I had sold my soul to Satan, and he wasn't about to give up wanting to keep me for himself to take to hell. I was torn between two lovers, physically and spiritually—my husband and my lover, and God and Satan. The parallels are ironic. I remember not really being able to put into words to tell my daughter what was happening. She saw her mum, who was lost and, at her young age, was also fighting for me. God had people strategically placed everywhere.

I had gone back to my lover to see him, and how he treated me was more than cold. I can see God's hand in that act. I remember driving home that day, barely able to drive from the tears and the heartbreak. It was at rock bottom, and I was suicidal. God had his hand on me yet again. I was in the mobile home on our farm property and was pacing up and down by myself, screaming in mental pain. I just wanted to die. I could not take one more ounce of heartbreak. It happened to be a Sunday morning. There was no one I felt I could talk to except the one person I had put a little trust in, and that was my counsellor Wyley Hargraves. The fact he was there when I called, I know that was God pursuing me. I was suicidal. I had just had my heart broken again.! I don't know what or if Wyley had anything on that day to attend to, but for about an hour, he spoke into my heart. I see now that God was using him to show me the love of Jesus. He calmed me and didn't leave me until he knew I was in a place in my mind where I was alright. The pain didn't stop, but my mind was calmed down. Wyley had prayed for me, and I know God heard his prayers. I got off the phone, and something from deep within my heart was crying out.

I could feel myself wanting to cry out to Jesus, but it was like I couldn't get the words out. I had been worshipping Satan. The lies filling my head were saying, 'You can't pray! You don't know how to! God won't accept your prayers, you worthless piece of adulterous garbage!'

The fight in my soul was raging. I started saying to myself, *I don't know what to say*, and I came as I was with three small but powerful words, 'Please help me.' Then I said it again. 'Please help me! I don't know how to pray anymore.' All I could do was keep repeating the same words. God never gave up on me. He saw what the world saw as worthless, and not for a second did He stop fighting for me. All I needed to do was call out to him. I needed the faith of a mustard seed, and honestly, it was all I had. He heard my prayer. Please help me.

··· 16 ···

The Resurrection

Saying those three words started what was a fierce battle for my soul. Satan was not about to let go of me just like that. Issues got harder. Temptations increased. Satan knew exactly what he needed to do to try to keep me with him. I had my husband still battling for me and not giving up. I had lost my lover and was craving the need to feel wanted, so I ended up contacting the Sydney guy again! Yes, I know; it's what pain does to you if you don't have Jesus. You go back to where you were struggling, but you usually fall harder.

I felt like I had no one. I wasn't involved in a church. I didn't want to tell anyone what was going on or the battle I was dealing with, so I tried on my own. I called a support group S. A. I got in contact with some people who I thought would be able to help me, but it was all about meetings. Some of the people I spoke to had been in this group for years, and I thought to myself, *I don't want to be stuck in a group where I couldn't somehow be receiving total freedom.* It seemed like these people had replaced their addictions with the group meetings. It was just a Band-Aid on top of deep issues.

I wanted Jesus, but I wasn't going to go to church. I kept falling in sin and hated myself for it. I wouldn't tell anyone about my sin because I was already struggling with adulterous thoughts. If I admitted to doing wrong id be labelled for good. I remember thinking, *If I get through this, and I get to the point of being there for someone else who has to work through addictions, then I want to be there for them.* I needed someone who wouldn't be judgmental but also encouraging. I hated that I couldn't just come straight from the life I was living into totally being restored. It's given me a heart of compassion for others that go through addictions.

I spoke with my counsellor, and he suggested that I go to an alpha course at a church I had never been to. At first, it scared me to walk into a church. I had not been in a church since everything that had happened all those years ago. I walked in, and my heart was racing. I felt so uncomfortable. I wanted to leave straight away, but I met a couple of people, Stuart and Joy. They made me feel welcome.

Even though I had known God my whole life, I felt like I had to relearn who He was. I was told in coming to this alpha course that it would help answer my questions I had about God. First, I heard a testimony. It spoke deep into my heart. As the night went on, I sensed God wanted me to give my heart back to Jesus. Most of the group had left except Joy and Stuart. I asked if I could speak with them, so we went to a room, and I shared my story from the last eight years. I was scared, but since I didn't really know them, it felt good just to let everything out of my heart after all this time.

Afterwards, Stuart asked me if I wanted to give my heart back to Jesus that night, I said I did, so we went through some prayer confessing and repenting of sins from the previous eight years. That night I gave my heart back to Jesus, but I never told my family or anyone at that stage. The alpha course went for a few weeks, and during that time, there was a camp for all the people who had done the alpha course. It was so encouraging. On the last day of the camp, I worked up the courage to share my testimony at the end of our last meal together.

I went home from that camp feeling amazing, but I was also very lost. There was no more alpha group. I didn't know what to do with my life now. I knew I still needed support as the temptations weren't stopping. My life went through a few weeks of going backwards because I had no one to mentor or disciple me. It was still my choice. It went backwards, but I remember crying out to Jesus to please find someone to help me. There was a particular day when temptation was so strong, and I gave in and felt bad spiritually. Afterwards, I hated what I had done. I felt like I was never going to be able to break the battle of addictions. Well, that's the lie I was telling myself as I spiralled into a downward mess.

I had started walking again after a long break, and one particular day I felt so broken about myself. I wanted to rid myself of me. Jesus was who I wanted. I fell down by the side of the road right next to a busy freeway on my knees and cried out to Jesus with an almighty cry from the depth of my soul like never before.

'Please, Jesus, forgive me.' The cry came from deep within my heart of realising what I had done. Where I fell on my knees to the ground was ironic because it was the same freeway where I wanted to run out naked and take my life. Here I was, down on my knees beside the busy freeway asking Jesus to forgive me because now I wanted to live and live for Him. That was a significant time because of what happened in my heart. At the alpha course, I meant the prayer, but I didn't feel a deep repentant heart was there yet.

You would think by now, Satan would have given up trying to get me back, but the situation seemed to intensify all the more. My husband and I were still separated. I was still living in the mobile home on our farm property. One particular night, the battle was on, and it was a battle for my soul!

All night I lay paralysed. My phone was on the bedside drawer beside me, but I couldn't lift a finger. I was pinned to my bed by demonic forces. My bed was soaked with sweat to the point it looked like I had wet the bed. Evil spirits had my body pinned. I had been having a nightmare that went on all night. I still remember all the details four years later. In the nightmare, I saw demons and angels battling for my soul. It felt like it had been going on for days, and the demons were winning. Satan was doing everything to try to keep me out of God's kingdom. He did not want me back with God. He wanted me bound and wanted me going to hell.

But God, in his warrior self, was not giving up his pursuit of me. With an almighty roar, the angels came with their mightiest strength and fought like I had never seen in my life. I had seen battles on television before, but nothing matched this one. I was frightened to death from the experience because I had not seen anything like this. At the end of the battle, the angels had won, and the demons were fleeing. I woke up but could barely open my eyes. I was shaking.

As I looked up, there was an angel slightly bent over my bed, looking at me. The angel didn't have wings. It just had what I would describe as a white robe that went to the ground, and it looked like something tied around its waist. The angel grabbed my hand as if it had pulled me out of being pinned down. I could hear a song. The angel spoke the words and said, 'Don't you worry, child. Father said, "Heaven's got a plan for you." ' I don't ever recall knowing this song, but the words have never left me to this day. No one but God and I know what I experienced that day.

As the angel took my hand and helped me up, the angel led me to my bathroom, and I looked in the mirror. I looked at myself in the mirror and saw a totally sweat-drenched person and the angel in the mirror as well. The next minute the angel was gone, but the words to the song kept playing over and over.

After that, I felt like I was in a daze, wondering what the heck had I just experienced. I was scared because what I experienced was real. There were no two ways about it! I went over to the farmhouse to tell my husband what had just happened. I was still trembling with fear and shock from my experience.

I believe in my heart that a mighty battle went on that night. I am here today to tell my story, and this was part of it. God will fight for us, no matter what. He will climb the highest mountain and swim through the deepest ocean for us. He did it for me, and He brought me back to Himself. I had never before experienced his love like this. A fierce and unconditional love! It brings tears to my eyes to think about this battle he fought for me. He stopped at nothing to bring me back into His arms again. There is no deeper love than this. This is Jesus, the lover of my soul.

••• 17 •••

Healing, Layer by Layer

After the dream, it was as if something in me had changed. There was something in me that felt lighter. It felt like whatever had hold of me no longer did, and like darkness over me had been lifted.

I wanted to return home to my family and live with them again, so after months of being separated, I did. My husband loved me unconditionally, and this was a major part of me wanting to return to God. Our children had been asking both of us to go to a church again since the moment we left the church eight years prior. I can honestly say my children played a big part in me coming back to God with their constant prompts and questions. I'm truly thankful for the love of all four of my children.

We started going to the church our children had gone to for their youth group. I really struggled. I knew I needed to be in a church, but the fear overwhelmed me. My biggest fear was rejection. The fear in me did not want me to be in a church. It reminded me so much of my past hurts. To make things harder, I felt all alone, battling a lot of internal thoughts when I first started going back to church. For a long time, every week, I would come home crying after church. It honestly felt like I was never going to fit in.

There was one lady in this church who took me under her wing. Her name was Christine. It was the simple little gifts she gave me at times and little things she did that spoke to my heart. She gave me a teddy bear that said, 'Jesus loves you.' I remember crying, just needing to see those words written had a beautiful impact on me. I think if it wasn't for her, I would not have had the courage to stay at church. It only takes one person to touch a life, and she touched my life.

In a Bible study group, I had begun attending another church through my counsellor's advice, and I met another friend named Fiona. She became like a rock to me. She never judged me. She loved me, unconditionally. I could go to her about anything and know I could trust her. She could see I still needed deeper healing and release from many of the spirits I had been connected with. She took me to a lady who did a prayer ministry, and I shared my story. This lady had tears in her eyes, and she was praying for me. She prayed for generational curses to be lifted, and she prayed those spirits out of me. What I saw was what looked like this black vapour come out from deep within me. It scared me, but I knew in this act of prayer, I was being freed from Satan's hands.

After the alpha group, I was longing for a deeper connection with people. I was put into a Bible study group in the Berwick Church of Christ through my counsellor. Through this group, God did some truly amazing transformation in me. I was told about a course that was called 'Growing to Maturity' (GTM). The pastor, Ken, with the Holy Spirit's help, had designed these GTM courses. I started going to GTM 1 with the other women in my Bible study group. It consisted of eight weeks, and it talked about understanding who I was, acceptance, hearing God's voice, repentance, and faith.

Then came what they called the 'Freedom Weekend'. I had no idea what to expect. I felt a little sceptical as it was new to me, but something deep in me felt this would do something for my life I had never experienced. I had battled with acceptance my whole life. All I had known was rejection. In my past, I knew of God, but I felt it was more of a religious act I was living, not about having a relationship with him. Then there was the Holy Spirit. I knew of the Holy Spirit, pretty much that He was the one who convicted people, but that was my limit of knowing him. I started experiencing the Holy Spirit and learning more about Him.

During the Freedom Weekend, there were a lot of prayers and spiritual healing going on. I used to think spiritual healing was just for people who were charismatic. My background was to run from this type of thing, as I was taught that it was evil. I had to choose on this Freedom Weekend if I was going to embrace who the Holy Spirit truly was and allow him to work in my heart as he needed. It came to near the end of the Freedom Weekend, and I had two people, Stuart and Fiona, praying with me.

To start, they asked me what the Holy Spirit was showing me. Initially, there was nothing, and I felt uncomfortable. Then, like a rushing wind, I saw something about when I was conceived, and my parents didn't want me. I saw a beautiful picture I'd never seen before. The Holy Spirit was there and was filled with the delight of me being conceived. It shocked me. When my parents didn't want me, He did. I never knew this. It brought tears to my eyes. He showed me that *He* wanted me.

When I prayed, I had to ask God for forgiveness for believing that I was never wanted because although I wasn't wanted by my parents, I was wanted by Him. I had chosen to believe I was never wanted. What a heavy burden I had carried my whole life, and finally, it was number one of being set free. Then the Holy Spirit took me to when I was born. He was there again, so excited about the anticipated birth of me. I saw him smiling and rejoicing over my birth. When my dad wasn't there, He was, waiting for his princess to be born.

Then the Holy Spirit took me to the memory of me with my dad on the train ride home where my insides were throbbing with the heartbreak of feeling abandoned. He was there. Jesus was with me. He had his arm around me, too. He felt the throbbing in my little heart and how it was breaking, but I just didn't know it. I had carried that abandonment my whole life. I asked for forgiveness for believing in that lie and was set free.

The Holy Spirit then took me to the memory in the playground, where I was under a seat curled up in a ball, hiding from friends because I didn't want to be teased. My broken heart from being rejected by other children was cutting me deep, but Jesus showed me he was there with me seeing all that was happening. He never left me. What a beautiful Jesus He is.

The Holy Spirit then showed me the memory of when I was cutting myself. When the pain was so deep, when I thought no one cared or loved me, and I wanted to end my life by cutting myself, He showed me He was there holding my hand. He was there fighting for me to live.

He then took me to the time I was raped. He saw me crying in the lounge room when I wanted to ring the police but didn't. His arms were wrapped around me, loving me. He then took me to the different people I had been with sexually when I was being used. He showed me how He was protecting me from things I could not see. In my sin and brokenness, He still loved me. That is enough to break any heart into a pool of melted love.

Then came freedom from soul ties. Whenever a person is with another person sexually, a soul tie is created, tying you two together and keeping a part of them with you. The Holy Spirit led me through prayer, and most soul ties were broken, some not, but I will talk about that later. The Holy Spirit took me to many places that weekend from my past to heal me. I received a lot of freedom from past hurts. Not all areas of my life were healed then, but it was the start of Jesus freeing me, the start of Him moulding me into the person He created me to be.

The Bible study group I was in at the Berwick Church of Christ consists of the most beautiful souls. They all just blanketed me with their sweet Jesus love and loved me unconditionally. There was one beautiful lady there named Katherine, who had such beautiful love towards me. I looked at her as a spiritual Mum, and she was beautiful to me. Then came Glenda. I cannot express in words what this lady means to me even today. I would not be who I am without her love. She believed in me all the time! Her love for Jesus shone through like a beautiful bright morning star. Its people like these who inspire me and move me to do and be who God created me to be. I never believed I needed healing from all the past hurts as I did, but with it came immense freedom in Jesus. It was like dropping off a truckload of concrete in one stop. I felt lighter and free.

It came to the part of the course where they talked about baptism. I had been baptised twice before, once at nine years old and again later in the church I left. But I felt the Holy Spirit call me to be baptised again. To start, I was pushing the thought away because of fear. All I could think about was other people and what they would think. I tried to push the thought away, but it wouldn't go.

Something in me felt like I truly wanted to be sincerely baptised and cleansed from my horrible past. So, I decided to be baptised again, but I didn't want anyone to know. I told my husband. My counsellor advised me to tell my children. With the help of Jesus, I received the courage to tell my children just two days before my baptism. They all came, and I was baptised by my counsellor and his beautiful wife.

This time when I was baptised, I asked Jesus for His spiritual gifts from the Bible, but I asked without fear. I left that prayer in His hands and just waited for Him to answer. For the healing I received, I praise God with all my heart. I praise Him for his great love He had for me in never giving up and never leaving me despite all my brokenness.

••• 18 •••

Finding Who I Am in Jesus

I have always had the heart to evangelise. It had just been buried for many years and obviously wasn't active in the time I had not been walking with God. One of the first things I thought about doing was re-engaging an Instagram account I had previously started (for the wrong reasons) and using it for the right reasons, namely to reach out to the lost souls in the world. My conviction right from the start when I opened the account was that there would not be anyone allowed to follow it who I knew in real life. To this day, it's how I have kept this account. It allows me to speak freely and be who I am without judgment. I share my everyday struggles, how I get through my walks with God, and what I need to do to keep going in my day-to-day time with Him. This account has led to many openings from God in numerous ways.

Something in my life that I realised had an impact was the pastor of the Berwick Church of Christ, Ken Raymont. Ken had a love in him that only came from Jesus. I had a warped idea of what a pastor looked like because I had experienced some bad times with some pastors in my past, but with Ken, the fact that he talked to me shocked me. I had believed for years I was unworthy to be talked to as a normal woman. This love in a person only comes from someone who has the heart of Jesus. Initially, I thought maybe it was just a one-off, but Ken gave me time, and I have lost count of how many times God used Ken to deliver me from other issues that would arise. He had a heart that cared for people and the spiritual well-being of their souls. I was never just a number. I was never just shoved aside like I didn't matter. He had the heart of Jesus. Ken wanted to disciple me and others, so in turn, we could be equipped to go out into the world and disciple others. That is what God intends. The church should be a place to equip people to go out into the world and bring the lost souls in and repeat the cycle.

After I had finished doing GTM 1, Ken had designed a couple more courses that eventually led me to where I am today. In the second course, I learnt how to start saying yes to God again. For eight years, I had lived my life my way. My heart needed to be retrained to learn obedience. Then, the next area I was petrified to learn about was the Holy Spirit. I only ever knew that the Holy Spirit was who convicted you. I knew nothing more than that until this time in my life. Fear had stopped me from wanting to understand more about the Holy Spirit. I had learnt so much about the Holy Spirit, but it came to the point where I had to make a decision to believe what I saw and was taught through God's Word, or I would run again.

I had never thought about the fact that I had chosen to sin and not believe in what God's Word had said about the Holy Spirit. I remember going home and thinking deeply about the Holy Spirit. I had come to a place in my heart where I asked God to forgive me for not believing in His word, and I asked the Holy Spirit to give me what gifts He thought best for me, including the gift of tongues. A couple of days later, in my heart, I could tell I had received the gift of tongues, but I was too scared. I didn't want to try speaking in tongues. I went to one of the meetings a few days after I had received the gift of tongues, and while standing in the church, I felt an overwhelming experience of the presence of God.

I was in shock to start with and asked myself if what I was experiencing was real. Then, the next minute I could sense the Holy Spirit telling me to open my mouth and speak in tongues. I was scared to start with, and I laughed when it first came out. I never wanted my gift to be used in the wrong way, and so I prayed in tongues quietly to myself. It felt strange, but after the meeting, I would pray to God over the next few days, expecting it would have just disappeared, but it never did. Still today, the gift is there in me. Once I confessed my fear, my heart was ready to receive what God wanted to give me.

I had come to a point where I saw who the Holy Spirit was in many ways. He wasn't to be feared. There was a holy fear always to have as in reverence, but I learnt I could talk with the Holy Spirit. I could actually have a relationship with Him. I started learning about being spiritually naked before God. What did this mean to me? What did it look like to me?

Well, every time God showed me something in my life that I needed to give up in order to keep Him, I would relinquish it. Some things were not easy. No idols seem easy to give up at first. What I mean by idols is things that take a more dominant place in our lives than God does in our hearts. I am truly thankful for his grace and mercy because He seemed to do the stripping away over time. He is still doing it in my life today. He also would show me where unforgiveness was, and I would have to go to people who the Holy Spirit showed me that I hadn't forgiven and asked them for forgiveness. Two of these people were my parents. The Holy Spirit showed me I had not told my parents for years that I loved them. I struggled with anyone telling me they loved me.

So, I asked God what was happening in my heart, and He showed me I had bitterness and resentment there. I had to forgive them whether they forgave me or not. I remember the first time I said to Mum that I loved her. It seemed hard, but what it did to my life was let light into my heart in the dark places. I also had to learn to accept when others told me they loved me. That took me time. I didn't know how to respond to people expressing love to me, particularly friends on my Instagram account.

I had to let God come in and strip me of my wrong misconceptions about Him. I had to allow people back in my heart slowly, but still knowing that God would be the only perfect lover of my heart. I know some friends noticed I couldn't accept or express love back to them, but they kept loving me regardless, and over time, that started melting my walls down. I learnt that with God's truths and His love in me, I could say 'I love you', and I ended up being able to receive it after many years.

The stripping away required other things to be relinquished. One area was I felt prompted to burn all my lingerie—and I had thousands of dollars' worth. I think for quite some time, I knew God wanted me to, but my heart was still holding onto it because I wouldn't allow God to fill that part of my life and repent of it.

Once, I got up in the middle of the night and bagged up all my lingerie. As soon as the first light came, I lit a fire and never hesitated. I just burnt the whole lot. I felt relief, and I felt freedom. Seeing the lingerie was a constant reminder of my past, and it wasn't good for my marriage. Whether we know it or not, we can have possessions in our lives that become portholes for spirits to stay attached to our lives. We will not experience real freedom unless we rid ourselves of those items. The truth is material possessions do not make us who we are. I learnt I was who God said I was through His Word, and I learnt to stand on his promises.

Another area of my life God showed me I needed to surrender was my overeating. My whole life, I had struggled with that. I had put weight back on, and I had told God I was staying there because if I was big, I wouldn't have to deal with men liking me again. I could hide behind a mask of being big. God asked me to search my heart about this. I had never dealt with this eating issue my whole life. I had tried every diet you could think of, but I would always go back to putting weight on and never deal with what was going on deep inside.

God showed me my heart. He stripped it back to bare again, and what He showed me was hard. He showed me I went to food for comfort. It gave me a false sense of gratification but only for short periods of time. He wanted my heart completely healed here, no more hiding behind the lie of being big. I felt tired at the thought of going back on a diet again.

One day I had to see my specialist, and he made a comment to me about my weight. Initially, I was angry, but I knew deep inside what he was saying was right. Here I was trying to share Jesus with this man, and I was not living like I was meant to be in Christ. I left my specialist that day broken-hearted. I never told him. I had also had my doctor telling me about my weight, and it was an issue that just kept nagging at my heart.

So, I made a decision to lose weight again, but this time with a heart attitude change that God was going to fill that void in my life once and for all. I repented of using my eating as a comfort instead of going to God for my needs. The journey was very hard. My age was against me, and nothing seemed to work. I spoke with my doctor, and she told me about cutting out carbs and sugar. The thought of cutting sugar to start with horrified me, but I knew it was what I needed. This time things were different.

I had decided I wasn't going to kill myself by going to the gym for hours on end. I was going to focus on God. I did cross many hard times. I stopped losing weight, and I hadn't really lost a lot, so I went to my doctor, and she talked about fasting. I was horrified and thought, *Surely, you weren't expecting me to do this, too, God? I mean, I was already dieting, right, God?*

Well, He spoke to my heart and asked for me to give up even more. I think I cried. I thought, *I can't do this; it's too hard!* I started because I wanted to love God with all my heart, not just part of my heart. I was met with feelings of anger, hunger, and feeling sick. I had a headache initially. It was hard, but slowly over weeks, I started seeing the results of fasting.

I started focusing on prayer and not on my goal of losing weight. I ended up losing twenty kilograms, and that is where I am at today. I went back to my specialist one year later and walked in as living proof of the testimony of God's transforming love. It felt good to walk in there with my heart changed. My weight still isn't perfect today, but I am happy with who God created me to be. I realised I didn't need the perfect body. I just needed a heart that loved Jesus and a heart that was willing to sacrifice anything for God, no matter what it cost me.

There were other areas in my life that God would have me surrender, but as he asked me to surrender, I would, and I started experiencing deeper intimacy with God that I had never known.

... 19 ...

The Doors God Opened

Through the constant surrender, I saw God open windows of opportunity in my life so that I might shine his glory for his kingdom. I had learnt through the GTM sessions about how to share Jesus with people we came across in everyday life. It was at this point that God reminded me of a young thirteen-year-old girl who went doorknocking with her pastor sharing Jesus. That young girl was me! Jesus had revived the passion He had instilled in me as a thirteen-year-old. I had forgotten all about it. I realised the passion in me was still very deep, and my heart comes alive when I am out on the streets sharing Jesus.

Through my Instagram account, I was sharing Jesus and reaching out to people through social media. Jesus would lay certain people on my heart to pray for, and I remember at one stage, there were three women God told me to pray for. I started praying for them and not letting them know I was praying for them until God told me to. Then the day came where I felt led to tell these ladies I had been praying for them. All three ladies were going through some very difficult times, even suicidal thoughts going through their minds. God used me to help bring these women to him. On the day I was leading them in a prayer to give their hearts to him, I was hit with an intense migraine and vomiting, but somehow the Holy Spirit gave me the strength to lead these ladies in prayer and deliverance in some areas in their lives to him. This was all done through private messaging on Instagram.

It was nothing but a miracle to have been able to help these women because I could barely see because of the migraine, let alone type words on my phone, but Jesus made it happen. I had to excuse myself at times because of vomiting, and then I would come back and keep praying and helping these women. I praise God so much for this that he opened my heart to listen to pray for them. Today one of the women who gave her heart to God had her husband and oldest daughter also give their hearts to God.

I remember trying to find this lady a church to attend from the other side of the world. She lives in the UK. I saw God do something that was amazing. Social media is not always used for good, but it can be, and this situation is an example of it. This lady and her husband, even today, we are still friends through my Instagram account. I praise God for that.

Helping others through Instagram opened my heart to keep praying for opportunities to help others. I started up a different Instagram account to reach out to married people, and amazingly God brought people to my account. I would journey alongside them on their walks and their prayers, and we would pray and pray, sometimes for months. Through perseverance, I saw God restore a few marriages just through prayer and encouragement. I had the privilege of leading one man to Jesus through my Instagram account. Months down the track, he and his wife and daughter were killed in a car accident, so I praise God I was used to reach out to him.

I was contacted on my Instagram account by a pastor who lived in Pakistan. He kept asking me for three weeks if I would share my testimony in his church over Facebook Messenger. At first, I didn't want to do it, but he kept messaging me and not giving up. The Holy Spirit was pursuing me to do this, as well. The Holy Spirit's prompts for me to share my testimony got louder and louder. Fear had hold of me, and God was telling me to let go of the fear and trust him to tell my testimony.

I gave in and said I would do it. My testimony had to be translated, which was something new to me. Although I was not physically in front of the people, I was pretty nervous. I shared my testimony that night, and many souls gave their hearts to Jesus. I had no idea God was going to do that. It was the start of something amazing. God had many more plans. After giving my testimony, I started talking to the pastor's son, Karis and asked what their church was involved in. He soon told me about the orphan children he was looking after. He would rescue children from bombings or children who had been left abandoned on the streets. I enquired about where these children were living, and he told me in tents. I asked to see these tents, and my heart sank. I cried and could not believe my eyes. They weren't even tents— just rags and sticks! I was in shock! All of a sudden, I recalled a memory of me as a little girl living in a tent, and all I could think about was these poor children. I cried deeply to God, and I told Karis I wanted to help the children. I didn't know how, but I wanted to get them better tents to live in.

I started asking questions, and I saw they needed clothes also. I asked Jesus to help me raise enough money to buy clothes, tents, sports equipment, and a toy for each child. God laid on my heart to create a fundraising dinner. I had never organised anything like this before, but God walked ahead of me and made the way. What happened, though, I wasn't pre-pared for. I knew what God had shared on my heart to do, but others didn't. So, westerners were struggling with the trust issue, namely, was this real, or were these people just taking me and others just for a ride.

I knew my testimony. I knew how I had grown up—with-out much and living in tents. God had placed this dream in me to get these children tents to live in, but it wasn't everyone else's dream. I came across some very hard times. I had peo-ple struggle with the whole idea. I cried many times while trying to raise enough money. So many times, I would cry out to God to help me. It was hard not having people believe in me. I could have easily given up because of the backlash I was receiving. A lot of prayers had gone into organising the dinner right up until the last minute. I simply had to trust God that the dream He had placed in my heart was going to happen, regardless of what others thought. I held fast to the dream He placed in me, even through all my tears and heartbreak.

God came through the night of the fundraising dinner. God had provided many donations for an auction that was also held that night. To watch the ways God provided was nothing short of amazing. God raised over $5,000 that eve-ning. I was in awe of seeing God provide as he did. There was enough money to buy new tents for the children and clothes, underclothes, shoes, toys, and sports equipment. The day the children received all of it was spectacular. Although I never got to experience seeing the children get these things, I saw them live on Facebook Messenger. To see them smiling, to know now they aren't going to be living in just rags and sticks, blessed my heart so much. As I looked back over the photos of the last two years, I cried and was so thankful to God for all he has been doing.

I remember lying in bed a few nights after the orphans had received their tents and clothes, and my mind started thinking about the children's futures. I laid in bed talking with God, and I said, 'I am so thankful that these children have something better to live in, but God, what about the children's futures? God, these children don't go to school. God, I would love it if the children could have hope like other children do and be able to go to school'.

So, God laid on my heart to start a school for the children. What I didn't know was that the young man who looks after the children had been praying about this for quite some time, and when I approached him, he shared how he had been praying for the same thing. I think I nearly cried. We started praying, and we ended up organising buying a big tent we could use to school the children in. We rented some land and put the tent on the land for the school, and with God's help, we started a school for these children. We called the school Immanuel; my daughter came up with the name. It means 'God with us'. The funny thing was, it was Karis' baptismal name. So, God had a beautiful plan waiting for these children all along.

I was asked to share my testimony and, at different times, God's Word to the people in Pakistan, which is pretty much another miracle because I am just a mother and wife who loves Jesus. I was never equipped to preach or speak to hundreds of people at a time. It was all done through Facebook Messenger.

One of the times I spoke, it was out in a remote village, and quite a few people gave their hearts to the Lord. I was excited, but that night I laid in bed and thought, *Surely, God wouldn't lead these people to Him, and they wouldn't be able to get fed spiritually?* I cried because I don't believe in people just saying a prayer and thinking that gets them into heaven. I know we need disciples as Jesus did with his disciples. So that night, lying in bed, God laid on my heart to start a church in Pakistan.

We rented some land and bought a tent and started a church. I was praying about the name God wanted me to call the church. After speaking on Ezekiel 37 on the valley of the dry bones, God laid on my heart to call it 'Come Alive Church', because that's what God did that night to those people who were listening to the message God spoke through my heart.

The night I spoke on that message, one of the people who gave his heart to the Lord was a witch doctor. It was a miracle seeing the Holy Spirit touch people's lives as he did. The next time I spoke, the witch doctor brought his family along. His wife was also into witchcraft, and she and their whole family gave their hearts to Jesus.

Many times, God did and still does physical healings over there at times when I have spoken. It truly amazes me because here I am sitting in a chair in Australia—sometimes with a nice top on, but on the bottom half, I would be in pyjamas and slippers because most of the time, when I speak, it's the middle of the night here. God is performing miracles on the other side of the world in Pakistan. What an amazing God He is.

God organised many more events where he used my testimony to bring hundreds of souls to him over the last two years. I have felt like the most ill-equipped human to be doing any of this, but yet God wanted to shine his glory to show that He can use someone like me to achieve what he had planned.

After a while, God laid on my heart what I thought was just amazing. He placed it in my heart to raise $30,000 to buy land for the orphans. That was a huge ask from God, but he had placed the gift of faith in my heart to step out and ask him for this. I didn't know how it was going to happen, but I just prayed and trusted God that it would.

Within weeks of praying, God had touched two people's lives to donate the $30,000. But there were testing times ahead because it was one thing getting the money and another thing getting the money to Pakistan. I went through some very difficult times for a few months because of the school fundraising. A lot of things kept going wrong, but God would find ways. I cried a lot and prayed a lot. At times it seemed impossible, but God in His good timing—not my timing—would make a way. After a few months, God made way for the money to get to them.

I was so excited when they received all the money. I thought they would be able to put their tents on the land and live there. The children need their own land desperately, but then we found out that the government laws wouldn't let them use the tents, and this came at such a bad time as the children were being sexually abused. It has been breaking my heart. These children are like my children now. They call me 'Mum', and for any mum, no one wants this for their children. So, I was praying again and asking God what He wanted. He has now laid on my heart to raise $40,000 for a building for them. We will put the school and the church and place for children to live altogether on this land. Again, I have no knowledge of how God is going to do this, but I trust He will make a way.

The other plan God has laid on my heart is to start a centre for the women where they can learn a trade and earn money. I am incredibly pleased to say as I have been writing my book, God has helped us open a training centre for the young women in Pakistan. The training facility will be an amazing opportunity in many ways. It will help the young women to get off the streets, and also it opens the opportunity for them to be married as a woman with a trade is deemed more valuable if they can bring money in financially. In God's eyes, they are valuable, but sadly in human eyes over there, they aren't. So, I am in a place of waiting and trusting God at the moment, knowing in his perfect timing, he will deliver the $40,000 for a building.

On top of all this, God has placed a deep passion in me to evangelise. I have a heart for the broken and the homeless, which comes from my life. It puts compassion in your heart, like nothing you can experience. I go into the city, and I just want to pour the love of Jesus on these people. I quite often go up and pray and just listen to their hearts, and then I share my story. I sit back, and I watch Jesus do His work through me. There are times when I feel led to hug the homeless people because the love of Jesus just pours through me, and He wants to show people love through me. Wherever I go now, Jesus touches people's lives. I thought I had a deep heart for evangelising, but recently I had a scare of finding a lump in my breast, and God has done even deeper work in me. The fire He has placed in me burns deeper, and the urgency to reach out to lost souls lingers more deeply.

••• 20 •••

His Poetry of Love Found Me

There is something to say when God brings a situation into your life that literally sweeps you off your feet and changes your life. God, in all His refreshing love, did this to me in a way that has drawn me into him so deeply. One of the hardest things as a writer is getting out what's being said in your mind onto paper. The love of Jesus waltzed into my life through some beautifully written, God-breathed poetry. God used a person on my Instagram account to speak poetry into my heart. I had never been so whisked off my feet by poetry like this in my life until now. I believe God knew my heart and how to pursue me in such a way only He knew. Even though He used a person He gifted with this poetry, I saw Jesus in a different light than I had ever seen Him before.

I could hear all the questions swirling around in my mind. *Was Jesus really this person who loved so deeply?* At first, I didn't embrace and respond to the poetry because of fear and vulnerability. I stood back from a distance and observed the poetry. I prayed about it. I wanted to know the intentions of God through it. The more poetry that was sent, the more I felt the love of Jesus, but I had walls built up around my heart, and these walls had been there for many years. The person who wrote the poetry gently showed God's love through being patient and kind.

To help me understand more about who Jesus is, I was recommended to read a couple of books. One was about the lies we believe in and how they chain our hearts to not being free to have this deeper relationship with Jesus. I realized there were still many lies and chains around my heart that needed unlocking. The other book was all about the different personalities of Jesus. This book showed many Scripture passages about all these different personalities of Him, and honestly, I felt shocked because I think I had put God and Jesus in a box and not as a human being who had walked on the earth. I had portrayed God as being this unapproachable being on a throne. I hadn't thought of God as a father but deeper still as a loving father who wanted to lavish me with every perfect heavenly gift to guide and bring me up as his child. God didn't want the chains kept around my heart. He saw me as this beautifully-created woman who He had great potential for, but He needed me to step into my true identity. It was through the poetry spoken into my heart that Jesus started unveiling the real me, the Tracey He created me to be.

Through poetry, I began to see the different types of personalities of Jesus. Deep, heartfelt words that only He knew would reach in and pull out all the darkness that was covering my heart. The poems spoke about God knocking on my heart's door, about how He offered me love when I truly felt unlovable by the world's standards. I saw how He gave me opportunities to see Him through creation. I saw how his promises are true and that just maybe this deeper intimacy was worth stepping out in faith by taking hold of his hand and seeing what it would be like.

As I am writing this, tears are running down my cheeks because I see and know just how much He loves me. Jesus kept knocking on the door of my heart all these years. He saw the unlovable me but yet kept pursuing me. I cry at the thought of all I have done, but yet he still loves me. Nothing stopped the pursuit of his love. I know how hard it can be to love someone who has hurt you, but Jesus just kept fronting up. Deep in my mind and in my human flesh, I think, *Why did you bother Jesus when I did all I did to you?* But I know the answer now. I know He pursues out of love, and all along He's been pursuing me. I pause for a moment and realize He has been writing my love story all along, the most romantic and beautiful love story I could ever wish for.

In my mind, I wanted to check out this Jesus, who was being written about. I started laying all my questions out to God and testing if what I was reading was a reality of who Jesus is. I asked, *Would Jesus really come knocking on my door? Would Jesus whisper love into me in the morning? Would He still keep loving the imperfect me? Did I need to be perfect so I could be loved perfectly?* The poetry spoke of Jesus as this love that was so pure. Most of all, this poetry lined up with God's Word. I found Scripture after Scripture that spoke on all the different personalities I had missed growing up. So, I felt comfortable knowing this poetry was on par with God's heart and character. It had me so intrigued I just had to know more and test out the waters so to speak. I remember my first ever encounter of asking Jesus for something that seemed crazy and wild, but I thought, *I'm going to ask Him anyway.* What I asked was for Him to give me butterflies, the ones when you first fall in love, and they make your insides go crazy, and you feel lovesick. I laughed as I prayed this, and yes, I was a bit hesitant at first, but I stepped out I faith and asked. At the time I asked for these butterflies, I was feeling some rejection in my life, and I kept thinking how Jesus says I will give you the desires of your heart according to His will. This was a crazy desire, and to me, it was going to prove that in my whole time of pursuing other men, all I needed to do was run to Jesus in the first place.

I remember clearly the day that person sent me all these poems about Jesus. The person never knew about the prayer I prayed. I had butterflies going crazy inside me as I had never experienced. I had let my guard down and let the love of Jesus fill my heart. I was never one to ask for experiences because even up until this day, I know faith is to believe in what we cannot see and trusting Him. But I felt it wasn't wrong to ask Him for butterflies because I needed to feel his love that day and in a deep way that only He knew how. I was walking around my front garden on this particular day that I had asked to feel these butterflies inside, and, I kid you not, the whole front of my property was full of these gorgeous brown and orange butterflies. I'm crying as I'm writing this now because Jesus went beyond measure to allow me to experience this crazy prayer I had prayed. No human has ever done that for me! All the chasing I had done in pursuing other men to fill me with deeper love, and here had been Jesus this whole time. I had missed it because of my disbelief that Jesus could truly love me as intimately as He did. I cried that day and repented of my disbelief of who God truly is. It was the start of a most beautiful romance that has not ended yet, and I don't believe it will until He decides to take me home.

As other poems and God's Word were sent, or I read, Jesus and I grew closer and closer. I soon discovered that if I wanted to go deeper in my relationship with Him, I needed to let go of the things in life that were holding me back. Every lie that was buried He has been hunting out like a mighty fierce warrior. Any sin He asked me to repent of had to go, and the quicker I dealt with it, the deeper and more intimate I felt my relationship with God was growing. The things I would dare not ask God about because of lies I had believed in, I started asking Him. He started teaching me through His Word. I felt like the veil between us was dropping, and I was able to approach His throne and not live in an unhealthy fear of God, but instead in reverent fear. I love that He is patient with me through all because even today, He's still getting rid of the many lies I have deep in my heart.

What I discovered about God through the poetry was this— He had uniquely designed me and knew that poetry was going to be the thing that spoke to my heart to bring me into a deeper relationship with Him. I had hidden that part of me away in the romantic person I was because I had held onto shame. The romantic side of me was used for selfish reasons in my past, but now I use it for His glory. I'm not scared of being who He created me to be. As the lies were dealt with, I could start walking in His truth. I started facing fears I never thought I would.

I was scared of deep water in the sea, so one day, I decided to go down the beach and jump off the pier into the deep water while there five stingrays around me. That was the start of being free in who He says I am—a child of the King. I am His beloved princess. His daughter, He adores beyond comprehension. I am thankful to God for sending His God-inspired poetry into my life and thankful that God knew it would change my life to be in this deeper love with Him. God gave me a gift of writing my own poetry, which I now use to bless many others, all praise to Him. It's a treasured gift that is special to me that only God knows about. I write messages (poetry) and now know with confidence that He reads every word I write. I am head over heels in love with the lover of my soul, Jesus.

••• 21 •••

I Found Jesus

So, here I am at the end of my story, my life's journey all written out in a book. Eight months of writing and sadly in my time of writing I have lost two people near and dear to me: Phil, who has known me since I was eight years old and was one of the first ones to tell me I should write this book, and my dear friend, Katherine, who took me under her wing when I came back to Jesus. They are both home now in the arms of Jesus. I know they would both be proud of me getting my book out. I feel emotional finishing up writing it with tears in my eyes.

I found Jesus. Three little words with a big punch. Three life-changing words. Three words I pray will forever change the lives of all who read my book. My prayer is that the Holy Spirit will touch each person's heart either to want to find Jesus or to want to grow into a deeper relationship with Him as I am doing each day.

One of my earliest memories I have with Jesus was praying one night a heartbroken prayer for my parents to get back together. He heard that prayer and has kept all my tears. That prayer was answered back then, although things are different now, what I'm feeling and remembering in my heart was that Jesus saw the little girl and held her in the palm of His hands. He carried me, held me, watched over me, and never let me go through all I did and my denying of Him. He never let me go, not once. I look back over the last eight months alone and see how each day God has been bringing me closer and closer.

Rejection has been my biggest life struggle. Growing up with parents being divorced twice. Missing my dad, feeling rejected by both of my parents. Doing crazy things as a teenager just out for attention and wanting so desperately to be loved, wanting someone to notice how much pain my heart was in, and wanting to find the one person able to fix my broken heart and rescue me. I wanted someone to see when I was going through all my health issues actually to care and know and feel my pain. I wanted someone who saw what was going on in my broken marriage. I wanted someone to see my pain of losing my child. I wanted someone to see how it felt when I was alone after putting all four of my children into school. I wanted someone to rescue me when I was being used and abused and raped. I wanted to feel deeply and truly loved without a shadow of a doubt.

Those words,

'I found Jesus',

I want now to shout from the mountain tops.

I want to sing so everyone can hear me. I have found love, true love,

everlasting love that never lets go. Love that embraces

love that chases, love that rescues, love that guides, and gently pulls you up when you are going down the wrong road. I found a forgiving love. I found a love that sheltered me and protected me. I found a love that never abandoned me. I found a love that was faithful and true.

I found a rock that wouldn't move when the rest of my world was falling apart. I found a love that cared when I am unwell.

I found a love that met my every intimate need, as I never thought possible. I found a love that helped me to love those my flesh struggled to love. I found a love that was compassionate.

I found a love that was healing. I found a love that battled for me.

I found a love that kept loving me despite my imperfections. I found my knight in shining armour. I found a light that lit up my darkness.

I found a love that didn't think I was invisible. I found a love that thinks I'm beautiful.

I found a love that loves all my scars. I found a love that is never blind to my needs. I found a love that provides beyond measure.

I found a love that reads all my messages when many others wouldn't. I found a love that cares. I have found a love that listens.

I have found a love that loves how I look, and He loves all my curves. I have found a love that cherishes me, no matter what.

I have found a love that finds me behind closed doors with tears in my eyes and holds me until they stop. I have found a love that talks to me at any time of the day. I have found a love that is interested in all my hobbies.

I have found love when my heart is broken. I have found a love that loves every detail about me.

I found a love that meets me in my garden and shares intimate details of his creation with me. I have found a love that loves the not so perfect pictures I draw.

I have found a love that is excited in me and never bored. I have found a love that loves romantic me. I have found a love that loves me unconditionally, and that is something that will never be found in any other human.

There lies the answer to my life's story. I was looking for all of this in everything in the world but was continually let down. It has only been since He has done great work on my heart. With each day that comes along, He asks me to surrender yet something else, my love with Jesus grows deeper and deeper.

All that I have been through has moulded me into the person I am today. Yes, I deeply regret a lot of decisions I made, but I know God turns all things from our pasts into good, so He will be glorified. Every wrong turn I took, He had an alternative path in place. He waited patiently and so lovingly. No one will ever know truly what the love of God has done to my heart. Some verses He just gave me as I come near to finishing my story are from Isaiah 61: 1-3.

> The spirit of the sovereign Lord is on me because the Lord has anointed me to proclaim the good news to the poor. He has sent me to bind up the broken-hearted, to proclaim freedom for the captives and release from darkness for the prisoners, to proclaim the year of the Lord's favour and the day of vengeance of our God, to comfort all who mourn, and provide for those who grieve in Zion—to bestow on them a crown of beauty instead of ashes, the oil of joy instead of mourning, and a garment of praise instead of a spirit of despair. They will be called oaks of righteousness, a planting of the Lord for the display of His splendour.

This is my heart; this is my calling. This is the journey God now has me on to help others who are broken-hearted and to help others who are still bound in fear and are not doing what God has planned out for them. My heart is for the poor, and I have a deep compassion God has placed inside me through the life I have lived. I have truly found Jesus. My prayer is that anyone who reads this book may also find the only one who will love you like no other, and that is Jesus.

About the Author

Tracey Brough has her heart set on eternity, wanting to set people free from the fears binding them. She mentors others by helping them see who God created them to be. She helps those trapped in depression by giving them hope through her own story of transformation. Tracey struggled her whole life, not knowing who she truly was and how much God truly loved her—until now. She shares how others who feel unloved and unacknowledged can live a full life being transformed by the love of Jesus.

Tracey Brough regularly shares on Instagram her day-to-day issues and inspiration. Her viewers and readers get to see a transparent person living in the real world. She also shares her stories via social media. God has been using her testimony in an amazing way in Pakistan. Through the sharing of her written testimonies, God is bringing many lost souls to Him.